REFLECTIONS ON
LEADERSHIP

WHAT LEADERS SAY ABOUT LEADERSHIP

Dennis Mossburg

Grey Moose Leadership Group, LLC
Spokane, Washington

Look for these books by Dennis Mossburg, published by Grey Moose Leadership Group, LLC:

Frequently Asked Questions. A Guide to Your Business Adventure

Dogs, Morning People and Other Humans. Essays on Sarcasm and Gratitude

Reflections on Leadership by Dennis Mossburg

Published by Grey Moose Leadership Group, LLC, POB 1383, Airway Heights, WA 99001

© 2020 Dennis Mossburg

All rights reserved. No portion of this book may be reproduced in any form without permission from the publisher, except as permitted by U.S. copyright law. For permissions, contact: grey.moose.publishing@gmail.com

Cover by florfi

ISBN: 978-1-7344709-2-5

First edition

To my darling wife,
Margo Mossburg,
who helped make me the man I am today,
and seems a little annoyed about it.

Foreword

Many great things have been said about leadership, yet there are a lot of people who do not know what it is or what it looks like. There are different styles and theories. Some of us worked in authoritarian environments where workers were treated the way W.C. Fields treated children, that is, seen and not heard. Many managers and business owners felt that workers should be happy just to have a job.

The sum total of leadership theory could be summed up as "Do as you are told."

Slowly, that theory has been falling out of fashion. In the modern era, B. F. Skinner was one of the first psychologists to suggest that positive reinforcement may be a better way to get the most out of your staff.

Fred Fielder then came on the scene with his contingency model that suggested leaders should change their style depending on the situation.

Many other thought leaders have since stepped forward with their own theories on leadership.

As a student of leadership and leader for over twelve years, I have my own theories and thoughts on this topic. As a student, I am always interested in what others have said about leadership, so I began looking at leadership quotes. What began as an exercise in learning from modern leaders expanded to a search for the wisdom of leadership through the ages. I have found many from modern thinkers and ancient thinkers, such as Socrates, Lao Tzu, and others. Even though these people lived centuries ago, their thoughts are applicable today.

On the pages that follow, I have assembled a collection of quotes that I found profound and applied to modern thoughts.

I also provide my own commentaries about what I believe the leader is saying and how you can learn from it. One of the lessons I learned is that even though these leaders come from vastly different times, locations, and cultures, there are common themes to their wisdom.

Now it may be that I chose these quotes simply because I consciously or subconsciously recognized these threads and picked them out, so of course they share some common themes.

What it boils down to is that these are great ideas, no matter when or why they originated. Great leadership has helped our species survive for thousands of years. The reason there are some common themes is because we had to learn the lesson of survival again and again. Thus is the nature of man.

There are several ways to read this book. The first, of course, is to just read it like any other book: Start at the beginning and read to the end.

You can also pick and choose based on the originator of the quote. If you like Colin Powell or Eleanor Roosevelt, you can click the links to their quotes.

If you want to use the book as a daily devotional to leadership, then read one quote a day and my reflection. Most of my thoughts are about 400 words or about two minutes to read. This is perfect for people who want to begin or end their day thinking about leadership or looking for lessons in their own journey.

Some of the leaders are well known and will hardly need an introduction. Others are less well known, and I have included a brief biographical sketch and information about how they influenced their life and times.

I hope you enjoy reading along as much as I enjoyed compiling and examining these quotes.

Table of Contents

Foreword 5
John Taffer 13
John Maxwell 17
Colin Powell.. 23
Ken Blanchard 29
Lao Tzu 33
Simon Sinek... 38
Colin Powell... 44
Dwight D. Eisenhower.. 50
Sam Walton 55
Arnold H. Glasow 59
Steve Largent 63
J. Paul Getty 67
Mark Goulston.. 70
Jim Rohn 75
James Humes 79
Bob Chapman 82
Kurt Vonnegut... 87
Eleanor Roosevelt 93
Max De Pree 100
Harvey S. Firestone 104
Marcus Aurelius...108
William Arthur Ward...112
Brian Tracy..117

Colin Powell	120
Dwight D. Eisenhower	124
Bill Gates	127
George S. Patton Jr.	130
Eleanor Roosevelt	133
Martin Luther King, Jr	138
Abraham Lincoln	141
Theodore Roosevelt	144
John C. Maxwell	147
Henry Ford	152
Antoine de Saint-Exupéry	156
Sam J. Ervin, Jr.	159
General John J. Pershing	164
Admiral Hyman G. Rickover	167
Harry Gordon Selfridge	171
Warren G. Bennis	175
Diogenes of Sinope	178
John Zenger	182
Colin Powell	186
David Marquet	192
Colin Powell	196
Will Rogers	199
George Addair	204
George Washington	207
Socrates	211
Julius Caesar	216
Epictetus	221
Dwight D. Eisenhower	229

Michael Jordan	233
Klaus Balkenhol	237
Beth Revis	241
Patrick Lencioni	244
Reed Markham	247
Rebecca Aguilar	252
Winston Churchill	258
Ben Franklin	264
George C. Marshall	268
General Eisenhower	273
Claudius	276
David Hackworth	281
General Mark Welsh	286
Angela Ahrendts	290
Johann Wolfgang von Goethe	295
Robert Townsend	301
Mary Barra	304
Seth Berkley	308
Vince Lombardi	312
Walter Lippmann	318
Carrie Gilstrap	323
Acknowledgements	326
About the Author	329

REFLECTIONS ON LEADERSHIP

The greatest gift of leadership is a boss who wants you to be successful."

John Taffer

This is a sentiment echoed in many ways by modern entrepreneurs and business leaders. It taps into our desire to grow and be more than simply a nameless worker in a machine. It recognizes that people want to grow and contribute to society. We are, after all, social animals. We want to help each other, and we feel rewarded when we feel that we have contributed to our society. Leaders who recognize this do well to engage their staff and provide them the opportunity for growth and development.

Let's remember that this approach also benefits leaders. One of the first rules of leadership and business management is planning for succession. If you are not developing your future leaders, then who will lead when you are not there?

Recently I was traveling with a manager who works for the same organization as I do, but in a different division. I knew this manager, but not well. This car trip was our first opportunity to get to know each other.

For the first several hours of the trip, we had a good discussion about management and leadership. Our thoughts were very similar about how people in our care should be treated. After a few hours, she held up her work phone and said, "You are good luck. Usually this thing rings all the time."

"I'd say that it's more a testimony to how well you have trained your staff. They can function for a whole day without you."

She took the compliment with humility and explained that she knew that she was going to be traveling for training, so she had spent time with one of her staff, preparing him to fill in while she was away.

Either way, she was preparing her staff to be successful. She went on to confide that currently her office is experiencing a large amount of turnover.

As I said, we work in the same organization, but different divisions. In my division, we are also experiencing turnover, with much of the turnover due to staff moving on to other organizations. It turns out that most of the turnover in her office is due to promotions within her division.

She is training her staff to be successful, so successful that those staff are able to move on from her office. She is becoming the feeder for other offices in her division.

For her, it means that she is continually hiring and training new staff. She is unbothered by this; in fact, she was humble about it. She accepted that being a leader means wanting her staff to be successful. Successful staff will move on to other opportunities, that being the definition of success.

To her, it is the right thing to do. She is a leader, so training staff is her job. She'd be training them if they were new to her office or had been there for years. If she trains them so well that other managers want hire them away, then she has done her job.

As social animals, we benefit when others in our society succeed, so shouldn't leaders be invested in the success of their followers?

Action Steps
As a leader, you need to hold one-to-ones with your followers to build an effective rapport. Part of your one-to-ones includes conversations about your follower's goals, but

this need not take long. Take a few minutes to figure out what skills and abilities your follower needs to build, and together brainstorm a dozen resources for the follower. Narrow the list to two or three resources (books, training, seminars, etc.). Set a short deadline (a week or two) to achieve the goal (attend training, read all or part of the book). Have the follower report back, then reevaluate and start again.

Most of the work is done by the follower; you are there to assist and guide.

REFLECTIONS ON LEADERSHIP

To add value to others, one must first value others."

John Maxwell

John Maxwell is one of the modern thought leaders I spoke about above. He is well known to many, and some of you probably have read one or more of his books.

In this day and age, the word "value" is becoming one of those buzz words that people sprinkle into their sentences to make them sound smart. In terms of this quote, though, that's a disservice to the word.

The current business use of the word value means to give something of worth or utility. Human capital comes to mind. (Another of those words or phrases that are almost meaningless from overuse.)

To Maxwell, leaders want their followers to be so well trained that they can be successful without the leader. Human capital is the sum total of the skills, abilities, and knowledge of an individual, so any training the leader provides adds to that human capital.

If you have ever mentored someone, you know the thrill of watching that person grow and develop. You know that rush of dopamine your brain releases into your system as you see your mentee overcome a challenge they once thought insurmountable. You feel that rush because you are invested in that person; you have provided them with knowledge, wisdom, and guidance.

As a mentor, why do you do that? You don't invest in people you don't care about, right? In other words, you don't invest in people you don't value.

Would you experience the same rush of dopamine, of achievement, if you did not value the person? Probably not.

But valuing does not simply mean that you like being around someone; there's more to it than that. When we value a company, we have assessed what the company has to offer. We have run various tests. We know its revenue, its sales, and sales forecasts. We have looked at profits and losses. We know everything about its taxes and its assets.

REFLECTIONS ON LEADERSHIP

In Maxwell's terms, we have done the same with the person, though less clinically. We may enjoy spending time with them, and we may value their company, but we also value their skills and abilities. We value what they offer. We value their potential, even if the person does not recognize that value, that potential, themselves.

Being a leader, you have to know what your followers are capable of and how to bring those capabilities out.

Action Steps

Letting your followers know that you value them and their work means you have to know how to deliver feedback. Feedback, negative and positive, must be delivered as closely to the behavior you want to correct or encourage as possible. Waiting diminishes the impact. Delivering feedback days or even hours after the event distances the follower from the work and does not provide them with the appropriate connection to the event. Time makes the event less real and more nebulous. At the end of the work day, how clearly do you recall the events at the beginning of the work day?

When giving feedback, describe behaviors. Link the behavior to the desired outcome, then ask the follower how they can continue the desired behavior or discontinue the undesirable one. Specificity helps. Simply saying that a follower gave a good presentation is not enough; they need to know what you liked about the presentation.

At the close of a presentation you liked, give the follower specific feedback about the project. Your conversation might look like this:

"Steve, you did a really good job of keeping your team informed about changes during the project. That helps in completing the project on time and gives me confidence in giving you larger projects in the future. What can you do keep turning in good work?"

Describe the positive outcome. Engage the follower's cognitive abilities by asking for their opinion, which also makes them part of the success.

To provide negative feedback, simply flip the script:

"Steve, when you do not turn you projects in on deadline, it sets back several other projects, and we turn in our product late to the customer. This creates distrust between us and the customer. All of this makes me hesitant to give you other projects. What can we do to help complete you projects on time?"

REFLECTIONS ON LEADERSHIP

Again, tie the desired behavior to the feedback. Describe the negative outcome. Engage their cognitive abilities by asking for assistance and making them part of the solution.

Deliver both messages in a neutral tone. Resist the urge to add anything else. Let it be. If the follower wants to argue with the negative feedback, do not escalate and do not engage. End the conversation with something like, "no worries," or "it's all right," and walk away.

Engaging with the follower runs the risk of both of you becoming escalated. You entered the conversation with good intent. Do not allow their reaction to drag you into an argument. Your goal is to change behavior, not to get into an argument.

Your follower's goal is to reframe conversation. If they argue, they want to distract from *their* behavior. At best, they are trying to excuse the behavior. They want a reason to keep engaging in the behavior, rather than find a way to change the behavior.

At worst, they are trying to bait you into an argument. At the end of the argument, they can walk away secure in the belief that you are the bad guy.

If the direct report is responsive, there is no harm in expanding, but keep it short. The purpose of this conversation, whether positive or negative feedback, is to talk about behaviors.

Experts agree that workers need more positive feedback than negative feedback. The research varies from a 3:1 ratio to 5:1 and even 6:1. Whichever is the most accurate, it is clear that you should be using the positive feedback model more often than the negative model.

REFLECTIONS ON LEADERSHIP

Leadership is solving problems. The day soldiers stop bringing you their problems is the day you have stopped leading them. They have either lost confidence that you can help or concluded you do not care. Either case is a failure of leadership."

Colin Powell

This book contains quotes from many military leaders and several from Colin Powell. This particular quote is becoming one of my favorites.

Colin Powell first came to the attention of many Americans during Desert Shield and Desert Storm when he served as the Chairman of the Joint Chiefs of Staff. In 2001, he served as the Secretary of State for President George W. Bush.

This quote contains several gems. The first sentence would be enough to sum up leadership: Leadership is about solving problems. That's why we have leaders: They solve the problem of disorganization. Leadership solves the problem of lack of vision and lack of training.

Any problem in your organization can be solved with the proper application of leadership.

Powell is not done. He tells you a way to recognize when you have stopped leading: when "soldiers stop bringing you their problems." I'm sure I do not need to tell you that this is true whether you are in the military or not. One does not need to be leading soldiers for this to apply to them.

As a leader in any organization, if your followers stop asking you to solve problems, you have stopped leading them.

Again, if the quote stopped here, that would be enough. But he continues with the two reasons that staff have stopped bringing you their problems, and they're pretty simple: They either believe that you are not capable of helping them or that you do not care.

REFLECTIONS ON LEADERSHIP

Powell finishes up by telling you that if it is either of those two things, you have failed. That's blunt, but effective. And true.

Other quotes speak about trust, so I won't go into that too much here, but that's what this boils down to. In the situations Powell describes, your followers no longer trust you, because they feel you are incompetent or uncaring.

Incompetency can be overcome with training, experience, and wisdom. Uncaring ... well, there are not a lot of options for this. Your options pretty much begin and end with finding a job that does not require you to lead others.

If you are having a crisis of your own leadership and you really want to change your ways rather than find another job, then help somebody.

Helping somebody is the best way to get yourself out of a rut, any rut, especially a leadership rut.

There is a more subtle lesson in the format of the quote, and I have hinted at it. Simply in the way Powell has phrased the quote, he has given a lesson in leadership.

First, he states the rule: *Leadership is solving problems*. It is a straightforward statement with no ambiguity. Anyone can understand it, and few could argue against it.

Second, he shows you an example: *The day soldiers stop bringing you their problems is the day you have stopped leading them.* Leaders don't want to give just a nebulous idea; they want to give an example. They want to give you something to anchor the rule to.

Third, he offers a solution: *They have either lost confidence that you can help or concluded you do not care.* In these pages I have listed a quote that deals with this situation, but let's look at it for a moment here. If you identify a problem, offer a solution. Leaders have solutions. They may not always be the best solution, and through carful conversation with followers, the leader may refine their solution, but they went into the conversation with at least the foundation of an answer.

Finally, he tells you where the fault lies: *Either case is a failure of leadership.* Again, we will go into more detail later, but the problem lies with the leader. Regardless of which of the two solutions he offered applies, it is clear that any failure is a fault of the leader. This is freeing because it means that the leader does not have to look far for the person who will solve the problem. All they have to do is look in the mirror.

Again, the beauty of this quote is the simplicity of it, but that does not mean that it is simplistic. He has succinctly provided a wealth of knowledge in a few sentences. The solution he offers is simply this: trust.

If you want to fix the failure, you have to create trust. Somehow, at some point, this leader lost the trust of their followers. It could have been one event or a series of events. Winning that trust may not be easy and it may take some time, but it must be genuine. If it is not, your followers will sniff it out, and they will come to distrust you even more.

Action Steps

Identify a problem you want to work on, and apply the formula Powell offers. Identify a problem, show an example of the problem, offer a solution, and finally admit that as a leader, any problem with your team is your fault. You have to admit that the fault is yours, you have to believe it, and you cannot just give it lip service. On the plus side, if it is your fault, then it's your solution.

Write, not type, a 100-word mission order, using each of the four bullet points above (including bullet number four where you admit that it is your fault). Writing this is important. There is plenty of research that shows that your brain treats the written word as more real than the typed word.

Once you have edited the document to 100 words, you have a solution that is specific and actionable. You have something that you can use to guide yourself to improving your leadership and relationships.

REFLECTIONS ON LEADERSHIP

Leadership is not about you; it's about investing in the growth of others."

Ken Blanchard

Ken Blanchard is one of the great thought leaders in leadership theory. Many would say that he is *the* thought leader in leadership theory.

Servant leadership is the latest popular trend in leadership. These pages will contain many quotes that will not contain the phrase servant leadership, but the idea is at the core of the quote. I try to shy away from fads, for they are by nature a flash in the pan. At its core, though, the idea of servant leadership is too important an idea to disappear so quickly.

One of the problems with fads is that some people adopt them not out of sincerity, but out of an idea that if they are seen utilizing those ideas, they may win clients, but their adopting of the ideas has no grounds in reality. They do not believe in them at all.

All that being said, this quote reminds the reader that to get the most out of their followers, leaders must turn their attention from inside themselves to outside themselves.

I learned the most about leadership by coaching and mentoring people who do not report to me, people I have no direct influence over.

I find it difficult to watch people flounder with tasks or skills. I am a teacher by nature, so when I recognize someone who could use guidance, I offer what wisdom I have. I don't complete the task for them, and I don't spoon-feed them the answer, but I do show them where the answer may be found.

That I reach out to people who cannot offer any immediate benefit to me has often brought about unexpected support.

I did not offer the coaching out of a sense that it might benefit me. I only did it because I wanted to help, and yet I reaped a reward. The key is that I would do it regardless, because I believe in investing in the growth of others.

I cannot carry my organization alone. I am not the executive of the organization, and the organization is far too big for one person to carry anyway. The only way for any organization to succeed is through teamwork.

In teams, the only way for an individual to succeed is for everyone to succeed.

Action Steps

Mentoring your followers does not require a lot of time. You can do it during your one-to-ones.

When you talk to your follower about their goals, together work out the next step they need to take to reach their goal. Do not make this a large step; we are looking at small actionable steps here. If they want to get better at giving presentations, start with them joining Toastmasters or some other speaking club. Notice I did not say that they have to give a speech; after all, joining is the first step. Together, decide on a timeline for completion of that objective, and a date to report back, preferably at your next weekly one-to-one. At that time, plan the next step, say giving a speech.

If you do not have weekly meetups, you may want to set two objectives at a time, perhaps joining a speech-making club and ordering a book on giving presentations.

When that's done, start having weekly one-to-ones if you are truly serious about investing in the growth of your followers.

REFLECTIONS ON LEADERSHIP

A leader is best when people barely know he exists, when his work is done, his aim fulfilled, they will say: we did it ourselves."

Lao Tzu

Fairly little is known about Lao Tzu, although the name we call him by may not be his name, but an honorific. He is largely credited with writing the *Tao Te Ching*, although it may also have been written by several people. A good idea is a good idea, regardless who came up with it (this is in itself a leadership principle).

He may have been a 6th-century B.C. contemporary of Confucius, or he may have lived in the 4th century B.C. during the Warring States period. The bits of information that scholars agree on is that he was born and lived somewhere in China and that he had a hand in creating Taoism.

His writings are so powerful that rivals across the political spectrum all claim that he agreed with their points of view. Perhaps all of it is true; after all, Taoism is not a particularly rigid religious practice. Most forms of Taoism follow the principle of *wu wei,* to "act without intention." It advocates "naturalness, simplicity, spontaneity," and the Three Treasures, which are "compassion, frugality, and humility."

No matter what is true or false about Lao Tzu, we are left with a series of quotes and thoughts that undoubtedly came into being millennia ago and yet somehow still have value today.

Here, Tzu describes a leader who is so humble in his approach that even his followers do not fully understand the impact of his influence. If a leader is truly only concerned with success, then he does not care that he gets credit for his aim being fulfilled; all he cares about is that his aim *is* fulfilled.

The leader in this quote has invested so much in his followers that their self-confidence allows them to believe that they have done it on their own. As a leader, how busy do you want to be? Do you want to work long hours doing all of the work yourself? Do you need to be there holding their hands through every step?

The leader in the quote has not only instilled supreme self-confidence in his followers, but look at their confidence in him. He is so confident that he has chosen the right followers, provided the correct training, and successfully articulated his vision that he does not even need to be there to ensure success.

How many leaders do you know who can say that about themselves? Can you say that about yourself as a leader? Probably not. Too many of us want to be there to make course corrections, to pick up our followers when they stumble. We want to be there to make sure each piece falls into place, and if any detail is not how we imagined it, we need to be there to make it the way we imagined it, even if our followers' version is just as successful.

As far as the Three Treasures are concerned, all of them are manifested in the quote. The leader offers compassion by investing in and teaching his followers. He is not micromanaging or playing the authoritarian, as both of those management styles lack compassion.

This leader is being very frugal with his time and energy. He is investing both in his staff, but it is just the right dose of time and energy. Too little time and energy and the team does not achieve the goal. Too much time and energy and the team members do not believe they have done it themselves.

Without humility, leaders would spend their time standing over their followers, taking credit for their followers' work.

As a leader, do you practice the Three Treasures?

I am not suggesting that you adopt Taoism. I'm not suggesting that you adopt any religion; that's not what we are here for. But again, a good idea is a good idea. It would be fair to say that each of the Three Treasures is the foundation to servant leadership.

They even tie in nicely with Colin Powell's quote above. Without humility, a leader could never admit that they are wrong, and that they need to solve the leadership problem they have found themselves in.

Without compassion, a leader would never care to solve the problems of their followers.

Without frugality, a leader could dither on and on about their vision until their followers eventually tune them out.

Again, I am not advocating Taoism, but it would be wise to consider the Three Treasures when you are working with your followers.

REFLECTIONS ON LEADERSHIP

Action Steps

Go help somebody. Help somebody who cannot help you in return. Don't tell anyone about it. Repeat until you get the desired results.

Leadership is a way of thinking, a way of acting and, most important, a way of communicating."

Simon Sinek

In any organization, one of the first things to fail is communication. If you are not able to clearly communicate your vision, you cannot lead. You can try to lead, but if your followers cannot see, touch, and feel your vision, they will not be able to fulfill your vision. Leaders must be able to talk about the larger vision. They have to talk about the big picture in such a way that followers know they can reach it and want to reach it. Leaders have to think about the end game and be able to communicate that to their followers.

REFLECTIONS ON LEADERSHIP

Leaders act with confidence. Leaders should be vulnerable; they should admit when they are wrong. They should admit when they don't know the answer to something. Despite all of this, their followers should feel that the leader is going to get them through anyway. They have to act like their followers are important to them. And for real leaders, it's not an act. Leaders have to act in such a way that their followers know how important they are to the leader. And I don't mean in a meeting targets and achieving key perform-ance indicators kind of way. I mean in the sort of way that the followers genuinely believe the leader cares that they are taken care of. That the leader actually cares about their growth and development, that their leader actually cares that they are alive.

When followers believe this, there is no reason to track key performance indicators; the employees will just work hard for you because they want to.

For some organizations, vision, mission, and values are just something to put in their strategic plan so investors can feel good about who they are doing business with.

For true leaders, the vision, mission, and values actually have meaning; the vision, mission, and values are reflected in everything they do. Followers should be able to read these and say "that's my leader." Leaders act in such a way that followers know the vision, mission, and values are important.

If your followers read the statements and do not see you reflected in them, then your vision, mission, and values will backfire on you.

If your organization professes the value of "cultivate an environment of integrity and trust," yet one of the managers frequently gaslights followers, then none of your followers will believe the value, and they will resent the organization for not following its own values.

Leaders communicate clearly and in such a way that followers feel they are important. When they find out there is a miscommunication, leaders assume the fault is theirs and seek to clear up the communication.

Communication can be difficult, especially with people you are close to, and if you are a leader, you should be close to your followers. You must work on communication. Learning to communicate is an ongoing practice. Do not ever assume that you know everything there is to know about communication or a person's motives. Over times, walls may build up, and it requires effort from both parties to tear them down.

REFLECTIONS ON LEADERSHIP

Introverts and extroverts communicate differently, women and men communicate differently, and young and old communicate differently. Ideas are communicated differently across various media. Leaders are not expected to be fluent in all of these modes of communication, but leaders do need to be aware of differences and make allowances for them.

In marketing there is the rule of sevens, which says that you have to market your product to your customer seven times in seven ways. This is a rule of thumb. Don't expect to find research supporting this, but like most rules of thumb, it's based on some experience. Marketers understand that the message does not get through the first time, nor through just one medium.

Teachers know that there many learning modalities, many ways that people learn. Different learning experts will give you a different number of modalities, but there are more or less seven modalities. Coincidence? I think not.

If marketers know it takes seven times and seven ways to get a message across, why don't leaders make the same allowances for their followers? Especially considering that most organizations have some form of marketing component. This concept is not novel to organizations, but somehow it only applies to customers and not employees.

A leader's message is not going to get through with just memos and TPS reports. Leaders must communicate their message through every medium available to them, and they have to expect to reinforce the message.

Be the kind of leader who thinks, acts, and communicates differently.

Action Steps

I am a very direct communicator. When people talk to me, I want broad strokes. If I need clarification, I ask questions. I generally do not want details until I need them. I do not like small talk. For communications with task-oriented people, this communication style works well.

For communication with people-oriented followers, you need to take the time for the communication to develop. These followers want to know how the task benefits the people. Be prepared to answer these questions, and be prepared to talk about life outside of work, the weather, current events, and the latest television shows.

I am not naturally a people-oriented person. I have learned to work on small talk, even though it can sometimes be painful for me, just like it can be challenging for people-oriented leaders to talk to task-oriented followers. In this

REFLECTIONS ON LEADERSHIP

combination, the leader will find the follower to be blunt, maybe even abrasive.

Good leaders are self-aware and aware of their followers.

Find that follower you just cannot talk to and figure out why. It's probably a matter of communication styles, so experiment with your communication styles until you find the right one.

Every organization should tolerate rebels who tell the emperor he has no clothes"

Colin Powell

Yes-men are the bane of organizations, but many organizations still allow them, whether intentionally or accidently. Many organizations harp on the idea of fit, so much so that when I started my Master of Science in Management and Leadership program, I expected the textbook to be a single line of text in 96 point, old English font that said "Fit." I was very surprised to learn that fit is not as important as some organizations think it is. There were three sentences and one test question about fit in my whole program.

REFLECTIONS ON LEADERSHIP

Many organizations accidently encourage yes-men because they hire and promote people who fit with the management. They fit with the organization's management theory. They fit with everything the organization believes in. Sounds great, right? Until you have surrounded yourself with people who think, feel, and act exactly alike. Now you have an organization where everyone is afraid to tell the emperor he has no clothes.

Just because an organization ought to tolerate rebels does not mean that it will. If you are a rebel, learn to read the room. Theory and practice are not always the same thing. An organization that does not value rebels is likely to punish rebellion. Look for ways to rebel while maintaining a working relationship with your managers.

I can speak from experience that when organizations don't encourage their people to have opinions different from the opinions of management, the organization turns toxic. When everyone thinks the same way, no one is on the lookout for trouble, which is fine if there is never any trouble. But how long have you gone in life without encountering trouble?

When everyone thinks the same, then all staff are managed the same. That's fine if the organization is a healthy environment, but organizations that don't allow dissention are not healthy environments.

I've been in organizations that deliberately passed up employees for promotions and projects just to see how the employee reacted, to see if the employee said anything. You have no idea how many times I heard the phrase "I learn more about a person by how they handle disappointment than by any other way."

I generally agree with the phrase, but the organization used it as an excuse for promoting fit over ability. Or an excuse for promoting clones over independent thinkers. When everyone thinks the same way, there is no innovation. A lack of innovation has killed many well-established organizations.

I was having dinner with a manager who had left my worksite for a promotion at another worksite. The manager was due to return back to my worksite. We were off duty and were attending a training. I had thought that I had the kind of relationship with this man that I could speak candidly with him.

He was not certain how he was going to be received when he returned, so he asked me. I told him that people did not think he was approachable. His brow furrowed and slapped the counter with one hand as he leaned forward and said in a growl, "I am too approachable."

I sat back, a little surprised at his reaction. As I said, I thought I had the sort of relationship that I could speak to him candidly. His reaction had an effect on our relationship, and the relationship never fully recovered. Not only did he show me that he did not tolerate rebels, over time I recognized that he did not understand the impact his presence had on others, nor did he understand the impact of role power.

Managers often think that they and their followers have one relationship; they fail to realize that their followers view the relationship very differently. Role power, the power to bestow punishments and rewards, colors all interactions between managers and followers. Leaders recognize this truth and act accordingly.

As time went on, I became more cautious around this manager. Sensing something was wrong, he tried to remedy the situation, but because he did not understand the root cause, he continued to address the wrong symptoms.

For my part, he had already proven that he did not want candor. He had demonstrated that he knew all there was to know about leadership and was not willing to listen to the input of followers. I, having learned my lesson, did not offer any more help.

There may have been more that I could have done, but by my calculation, the relationship had reached the point of diminishing returns, and I planned my departure.

I told the emperor that he had no clothes, and I paid the price.

Action Steps

How to receive candor:

1. Assume a good intent from the follower delivering the message.

2. Be supportive of the follower.

3. Pause. Slowly count to five, ten if you have to, then thank the follower, even
if you do not agree with the message. Remember, you asked for it.

How to deliver candor:

Followers need to tread carefully. Even if you think you can deliver candor, it could backfire as it did for me. If you feel you can be candid, you must take the long view and deliver

REFLECTIONS ON LEADERSHIP

the message with as much tact as you can. If your manager has done a good job of building a relationship with you, you may be safe to take the risk. As a blanket rule, I would say do not do it.

1. Describe behaviors.

2. .Know your audience. Deliver the candor one-to-one. You do not want your boss to lose face.

3. Talk about one topic only. More than one topic may feel like an attack.

You don't lead by hitting people over the head
— that's assault, not leadership."

Dwight D. Eisenhower

Dwight D. Eisenhower was something of an expert on using force; after all, he was the Supreme Commander of the Allied Expeditionary Force in Europe during World War II. He graduated from West Point in 1915 as a Second Lieutenant. He sought action in World War I, and finally he received orders to take his unit to France. Unfortunately for him, the Allies had the bad form to sign the Armistice one week before he was due to report to France.

Between the great wars, Eisenhower worked for several generals, including Pershing and MacArthur. He was very

REFLECTIONS ON LEADERSHIP

interested in tanks and the role they would play in future wars. During this time, he also attended and graduated from several war colleges. For a time, he served on the faculty of the Army War College, once again preparing plans for future wars.

In 1935, Major Eisenhower accompanied General MacArthur to the Philippines, where the two served as advisors to the Philippine government in the development of their military. During this time, Eisenhower and MacArthur had philosophical disagree-ments about military leadership.

Many credit this experience with MacArthur as giving Eisenhower the skills needed
to work with Generals Patton and Montgomery, and Winston Churchill during World War II.

Eisenhower's military career is well documented as is his presidency, and there is no need to go into great detail here. The point is this: If a man who had over 38 years in the military said that you don't lead people by hitting them over the head, it gets your attention.

Some of his contemporaries criticized Eisenhower for never having served on a battlefield. Despite that, when it came time to designate one general to lead the largest amphibious landing in world history, a landing force that included troops from the United States, the United Kingdom,

Canada, and nine other countries, Eisenhower was the man they turned to manage the logistics, strategy, and personalities to bring it all together.

That required excellent leadership skills. When that man talked about leadership, many listened.

Part of his leadership strategy was leadership by walking around, though he would have hardly called it that. He likely would have just called it leadership. Eisenhower tried to move through the bases and camps and meet as many of the troops, from privates to officers, as he could. He remained positive, knowing that followers feed off the energy of their leaders. He also knew that often troops were not looking for awards; all that most of them wanted was a pat on the back and an acknowledgement of their hard work.

Eisenhower was not a great orator or overly charismatic, two traits people believe
great leaders need to deliver their vision. Those attributes help, but are not necessary,
and Eisenhower is proof of that. For over two decades, here was a man who (as a general or President of the United States), made decisions that impacted the lives of most of the world's population. And he did that with pats on the back, not knocks on the head.

REFLECTIONS ON LEADERSHIP

Action Steps

1. Build relationships with your followers. Build trust with your followers. Ask them real questions.

2. Ask them *what* and *how* questions.

3. What are your goals?

4. What are your hobbies?

5. What are your kids' names?

6. How do you spend your time?

Why questions ask for a conclusion and feel like an investigation. When people feel like they are being investigated, their barriers go up. They feel like they have to defend themselves. *Why* feels personal. *What* and *How* feel conversational.

Consider these two questions:

1. Why did you do that?

2. What led to that?

The first question presupposes that only one person was responsible for the outcome. Even saying it to yourself, did you notice your tone? It probably sounded accusatory. How have you felt on the receiving end of that question? The first question locks you in the past as you go on a journey of self-discovery to understand your motivations.

The second question asks for the same information, but it presupposes that there are many factors that lead to the end result. Some of those factors may have been due to actions of others, even others outside of the organization. The second question asks for root causes and helps you look at the future.

Some managers do not care about relationship-building. All they want are results. Your followers do not care about your results. They care about relationships. Give them relationships, and they'll give you results.

REFLECTIONS ON LEADERSHIP

Outstanding leaders go out of their way to boost the self-esteem of their personnel. If people believe in themselves, it's amazing what they can accomplish"

Sam Walton

Almost everyone knows or thinks they know Sam Walton, the founder of Walmart. Some people have strong feelings about Walmart and the retailer's business practices. My intent is not to argue for or against Walmart. I will point out that Sam Walton died in 1992 and can hardly be held responsible for the business practices of a company that has continued to function for over three decades after his death.

DENNIS MOSSBURG

Whatever his company is today, when he was alive, Walton developed exceptional leadership skills. One night he could not sleep, so he went to an all-night bakery, bought four dozen donuts, and delivered them to one of his distribution centers. While there, he spoke with his workers and discovered that the center needed two additional shower stalls. He had the showers installed.

Think honestly about your organization, especially if it is a 24-hour operation. When was the last time the leader of your organization showed up on the graveyard shift with donuts? When was the last time they showed up with anything? I am guessing it is probably not very often.

How quickly are facility plant issues resolved?

The trip cost Walton some gas, say $30 for donuts, and his time. He went out of his way for his people, and he provided them value. How long do you suppose those employees remembered this incident? Probably the rest of their lives. Walton spent one night out of his life and a little walking around money; in return, he received information about the facility and staff loyalty. You don't buy that kind of loyalty with a paycheck.

Do you think those workers worked just that much harder? What do you suppose those workers told the next shift of workers when they came into work? You better believe they told all about meeting the great Sam Walton. Do you suppose that next shift worked just a little harder knowing that Walton might someday show up on their shift?

What impact did the new showers have? It's hard to say, but imagine how you have felt when your boss made changes to the physical plant of your workspace, changes that you needed. Would you feel valued? If it happened right away, would you feel like the boss cared?

Think about a time you took a complaint to your boss. Did they act on your complaint? If they did, how quickly did they act? Did they offer you donuts as you were making your complaint?

This is one incident in Walton's life. How often did this sort of event repeat itself? It probably happened often. Thinking back on some of the managers in my life, however, if they had shown up on graveyard with donuts, the staff would have been suspicious and a few donuts would not have been enough incentive to speak freely. Donuts are not a substitute for a relationship; they are a bribe. Build relationships, and donuts are a bonus.

Action Steps

Do something unexpected for your followers. I do not mean have a secretary do something unexpected for your followers. I mean you! Go buy donuts for your followers and share the donuts with them. Listen seriously to their concerns. Find out the pain points in their lives and fix them. If you do seek out the pain points and provide excuses without solutions, your followers will doubt your future offerings.

If your followers do not immediately open up, that means you have to buy more donuts and actually, really solve more pain points.

REFLECTIONS ON LEADERSHIP

One of the tests of leadership is the ability to recognize a problem before it becomes an emergency."

Arnold H. Glasow

You may have had a manager who always operates in chaos. They run around like trying to put out one fire after another, little realizing that they are ultimately the source of the fires.

Too often this type of manager is too busy reacting to situations when they should have been proactive. This is a situation they should have been aware of, but they were so busy with other things they did not deal with it when it was a small thing.

Followers recognize this behavior. In most cases, they have even told their managers about this looming problem, but the manager was too busy to deal with it because they were putting out other fires.

I have worked in places that seem to value this type of behavior, even to the point of promoting those "leaders." To many managers, the type of leader jumping from one fire to another is a hero because they are busy putting out fires. This type of leader is often talking to their bosses and talking about their challenges. This gives them valuable face time with the managers. This, in turn, gives the managers the impression that this leader is hard-working, that they are getting things done.

Whereas to some managers, leaders who are not in a constant state of chaos do not appear to be doing anything. They are not always running around putting out fires. They are not constantly stressed out. Some managers think that because they are not constantly putting out fires, they must not be effective.

Perhaps your leader who is not always stressed, who is not always putting out fires, who is not always in a state of chaos is actually the better leader because they have trained their followers to deal with issues. They have listened to their followers and have been able to anticipate emergencies and

REFLECTIONS ON LEADERSHIP

deal with them before having to bring the situations to anyone's attention.

The problem with this type of organization is that the first leader is seen as a hero while the second leader is seen as lazy, but when you have all the facts, it is easy to see that the real hero is the leader who doesn't need the face time. The leader who seems to be doing nothing has, in fact, done everything they need to do to ensure their team's success and is now reaping the benefits by not having to react to everything.

Their deliberate actions are not as flashy, dynamic, and attention-getting as the first leader's reactions, so the deliberate actions do not gain attention.

Managers look for easily measurable targets. Sometimes the impact of deliberate training and coaching (actions that often eliminate or at least mitigate emergencies) is not easily measurable. Sometimes the only way to recognize it is by the lack of emergencies.

In World War II, the Allied military took detailed statistics about bullet holes in airplanes that returned to base. The bullet holes were overwhelmingly in the fuselage and the wings. Few returning aircraft had bullet holes in the engine areas. The military concluded that they needed to add armor to the fuselage and wings.

But a statistician correctly pointed out that airplanes that had bullet holes in the engine areas of the airplane are not likely to return at all. The Allies added armor to the engine areas. The end result? More airplanes survived and returned home.

Look for the lack of evidence as it may prove to be as useful as evidence.

Action Steps

Look at how you measure the leaders in your organization. Are you measuring the correct things? Do you have a leader in your organization who gets the job done, but does not need a lot of hand-holding?

Talk to their followers. Ask them about their leader. You may find that you have been measuring the wrong things.

REFLECTIONS ON LEADERSHIP

I think leadership is more than just being able to cross the t's and dot the i's. It's about character and integrity and work ethic."

Steve Largent

If you don't know the name Steve Largent, then you cannot consider yourself a Seattle Seahawks fan. He was the first Seahawk ever invited to the Pro Bowl, the first of seven Pro Bowls for the Seahawks receiver. At his retirement, he held every major NFL receiving record. At one time, he held the record for 177 consecutive regular season games with a reception. He was also the first NFL receiver to have 100 career touchdown receptions. He played for the Seahawks from 1976 to 1989, long before the Seahawks had a quarterback named Wilson.

With that kind of résumé, you would expect a huge personality, someone who drew attention to himself. Someone who was always in front of the press. You wouldn't be more wrong. As a player, Largent was humble. He didn't rely on speed; he relied on basics and fundamentals. He focused on catching everything thrown his way, and he was known for outworking the secondary with head fakes and cuts that left the defenders running out of their shoes.

He was the 1988 Walter Payton NFL Man of the Year, and the 1989 Bart Starr Award winner. The Seahawks also have named an award after him. The criteria for all of these awards are slightly different, but they are given to players who exemplify integrity and are outstanding members of their community.

You may not have heard Steve Largent's name, but he was one of the best on-field and locker room leaders the Seahawks have ever known.

We hear so much these days about micromanagers and toxic leadership. One of the chief signs of micromanagers and toxic leaders is people who tell you to cross the t's and dot the i's. It's a sign of control. It's a sign of perfectionism. It's a sign of insecurity.

REFLECTIONS ON LEADERSHIP

Leaders are not perfectionists. They admit their imperfections.

Leaders are concerned with integrity, character, and work ethic. Leaders have to be able to look themselves in the mirror at the end of the day. If they cannot, they are not acting with integrity.

Leaders are concerned with their character. I'm talking character here, not image. They have to be trustworthy. They exemplify their values. They talk about big ideas, not people. More than talking about those ideas, they live those ideas. Leaders are the example their team needs.

Action Steps

Honestly audit your daily actions. Do you yell at people? Do you talk down to people? Do you delegate work, just so you do not have to do it? Do you delegate work, then double- and triple-check their work? Or do you delegate work for actual growth and development opportunities?

Do you want your daily activities broadcast on the news? Or are you fine with others getting the credit? Do you tell people to do the work your way, even if their way gets the same results?

If you did not like the answers to these questions, look for ways to change your actions. Treat people with respect. Treat people as an end, not a means to an end.

REFLECTIONS ON LEADERSHIP

The employer generally gets the employees he deserves."

J. Paul Getty

Getty was a very interesting character. He was famous for being miserly, even refusing to pay the ransom for his grandson and installing pay phones in one of his homes. At the time of his death in 1976, Getty was worth $6 billion or about $21 billion today. Whatever you think about Getty, this is a good quote.

It is easy to think he is talking about karma or some other spiritual concept; while I am not ruling that out, there is a simple, tangible reason this quote is true.

If you do not treat your employees with respect, they will not treat you with respect.

If you only look at employees as an expensive line item, they are not going to be very loyal.

You need to invest time in your employees. You need to train them. If you don't train them and they don't perform up to your standards, is it their fault or yours? They cannot intuit your standards. You have to tell them, and you have to show them through your actions.

If they are good employees, but you fail to provide them training, advancement opportunities, raises, even a glimpse of a better future, they will leave you. All that you will be left with are the yes-men and the people who only work for you for the paycheck.

Train your employees and care for them, and you will get the employees you want and deserve.

Action Steps

Meaningful one-to-ones: One-to-ones are popular right now, but they are not meaningful if they are not structured properly. I once had a follower who was not fitting in with the culture. He had transferred to our worksite from another. His coworkers had a long list of complaints about his performance, and so did I. I had tried the typical strategies: training sessions, counseling sessions, and negative performance reviews. I even showed him video of his performance.

None of those techniques worked until I tried one-to-ones in which I allowed him to talk about whatever he wanted, work-related or not. Ninety percent of the meetings consisted of him talking about his challenges on the job and at home. To my surprise, the two were related. At the end of each meeting, I gave him actionable steps to take to improve both.

He was near the end of his career, and he retired before he became a "perfect" employee; however, he did show significant improvement.

"A leader who is confused or confusing causes too much anxiety, and a leader who is too controlling is revealing more insecurity and a lack of leadership."

Mark Goulston

Mark Goulston is a psychologist who has written several books about psychology and the workplace. He hosts a podcast and has appeared on many televisions shows.

How often have you seen what he describes? Your leader issues one directive, only to issue a contradictory directive a few days later. When you point it out, there is always some excuse.

"The rules have changed."

REFLECTIONS ON LEADERSHIP

"You misunderstood me."

"I didn't say that."

How can followers relax if they don't know what to expect from a leader? If they receive contradictory information or information that is not clear, how can they fulfill your vision?

I know that communication is a two-way street and at some point there is a responsi-bility for the follower to ask for clarification, but if asking for clarification does not lead to actual clarification, why bother asking?

At some level, the leader knows that they don't know what they are talking about. To gain some confidence in themselves, they look for things they can control. They look for things they have authority over. They start controlling their staff. They lack control in their lives, so they try to exert undue control over their followers.

They don't have confidence in themselves, so they exert extra control over their staff. They doubt their own abilities, so they doubt their followers' abilities.

If you have ever been told that you are a micromanager, you probably didn't believe it, so you didn't listen or take the information to heart. If you heard it multiple times, there may be something to it.

Consider some of these questions:

- Do you trust people to do their job as well as you can?
- Do you redo the work of your followers?
- When you delegate, do you give your followers a step-by-step process or an end goal to achieve and expect them to find a way?
- Do your employees take initiative or do they wait for you to make decisions?
- Do your followers ever come up with good ideas or are you the only one with good ideas? Always?
- Do your followers avoid you?

If these questions left you uncomfortable, you may be a micromanager. If you are defensive about it, you might ask why it's such a bad thing; after all, what's wrong with perfection? The quest for perfection is a crutch to cover the fact that you are insecure.

Employees leave micromanagers. Those who stay only work hard enough to keep you from bothering them.

If you want to stop being a micromanager, start by being more optimistic. Gratitude is big right now. Many people are keeping gratitude journals or finding some other way to acknowledge that good things have happened to them that day.

Instead of asking "What if?" ask "Imagine if?" That change creates a new perspective. The first question presupposes a negative outcome. The second question presupposes a positive outcome.

Do not look for fault in your followers; look for the good things they have done, then tell them about it. Do not use the feedback sandwich. The sandwich is an antique and needs to be retired. Respect your staff enough to give them unqualified praise.

Negativity bias guarantees that we will be tougher on ourselves than anyone else can be. As a manager, you do not need to pile on.

Negativity bias is a survival instinct we inherited from our caveman ancestors. Imagine a caveman sitting at the evening campfire chowing down on some delicious berries. If all he thinks about is how delicious the berries are, and he doesn't stop to think about the Saber-toothed tiger that nearly ate him, then he is not likely to survive his next encounter at the berry patch.

Learn to trust your employees, and your insecurity will ease and your leadership skills will improve. Employees who feel trusted will trust you. When they trust you, they will feel less anxious and they will relax. When they relax, they will provide a better product. When they provide a better product, your leadership will improve, because you are no longer so insecure and scared about their work. When you are no longer scared about your employees' work, they will begin to trust you.

We spend a lot of time worried about work/life balance without ever considering that if we treated our followers better, there would be no need for a work/life balance.

REFLECTIONS ON LEADERSHIP

A good objective of leadership is to help those who are doing poorly to do well and to help those who are doing well to do even better."

Jim Rohn

We are a disposable society.

My father-in-law and his brother were antiques dealers. I always enjoyed looking at the things in their shops; some of the items were over 100 years old. Some were well-used tools, and others were hardly-used knickknacks. All of them were well made, and most of them still worked.

There were 50-year-old sewing machines whose needle still bobbed up and down when you put your feet on the treadle. Old phonographs with the wax cartridges still offered the scratchy sounds of real instruments.

I have a 1950s telephone with a dial on the face. The thing weighs about 50 pounds. It still works and it's over 60 years old.

These things were durable and meant to stand the test of time. They were made out of metal, wood, and glass. They were made with care and sometimes had the maker's mark on them.

I cannot imagine what will be in the antique shop in 50 years.

Actually, yes I can; it will be the same things that were in the shop 50 years ago and there won't be anything designed and built from our time, because everything in our time is built to break, wear out, and stop working. Planned obsolescence.

Things are not designed to last. There's no money in it. Think of the rotary phone I mentioned above. It does one thing, two if you count it as a home defense weapon because of the weight. With my modern phone I can make phone calls, shut out the rest of the world, and probably launch nuclear weapons if I asked it nicely. When that phone

REFLECTIONS ON LEADERSHIP

is six years old, it will be horribly outdated. It may not even work.

When the old phone was new, someone paid the manufacturer for the phone, then never had to pay for another one. My modern phone will not be useful in six years, and I will have to buy another. And six years after that, I'll buy another and again and again. This is what business schools call an evergreen product. It's pretty cool when someone is paying you again and again for a product. It's not so cool when it's you buying something again and again.

I'm a little off track, but I am making a point: As a society, we are used to throwing things away when we become bored with them. When our cell phone no longer has all of the cool gadgets and whizbangs, we upgrade. It's what we do with everything, including employees.

I have news for you. You know how your phone can get updates? You can do the same with employees; it's called teaching, coaching, and mentoring.

Why are we more dedicated to updating phones than we are to updating people? How often have you heard people talking about having to download the latest update for their phone? Some people get excited about it. They can't wait to find out what new cool things their phone will be able to do.

When was the last time you heard a manager talk about having to send their people to training (upgrade)? They usually complain about it. They talk about the cost. They talk about the downtime. They whine about the new procedures.

Do a cost-benefit analysis of training and mentoring staff so that they improve their skills, so that you can keep them in your organization for their entire career versus the cost of hiring, training, and firing staff on a rotating basis.

Consider the fact that happy employees create happy customers.

Consider the stress you feel at having an underperforming staff member. Are you better off continually hiring and firing people hoping you get the right one? Or are you better off just investing time in your staff, so you don't have to worry about them anymore?

Help your poor employees do well and your good employees do even better, and you will see a synergistic growth in morale, employee engagement, customer satisfaction, your bottom line, and your mental health.

REFLECTIONS ON LEADERSHIP

One secret of leadership is that the mind of a leader never turns off. Leaders, even when they are sightseers or spectators, are active, not passive, observers."

James Humes

How many times have you heard about the long hours presidents put in? Regardless of your political thoughts, I'm sure you've noticed that U.S. Presidents are all reputed to put in long hours, sometimes waking up early to read newspapers or books.

This is not just limited to presidents. CEOs like Elon Musk work long hours, too, spending time reading and studying.

Leaders are always thinking about ways to make their team better. They look for tactics that work, even if the tactics are from a field other than their own. Leaders watch for other leaders. As a sports fan, I watch the captain of a team to see how they interact with their teammates. How they lead is different, but they do the same things.

When their teammates approach the boiling point, the team captain is the first one there calming everyone down. They are there congratulating the scorers, and consoling when someone fails. They're there to ensure their teammate's head is on straight.

Their mind is always working. They see all of the field, and they are working out strategies to improve.

Even when leaders appear to be passive observers, they are critiquing everything.

In my job, I am a defensive tactics instructor. I know how to teach people how to survive physical confrontation. I know how the body moves and how it should move to get the desired result.

When I'm teaching a class, I may look like I am a passive observer, but I am watching how people move, how they perform actions, and I can work out the end result before they have even begun the move. When they make an error, I give them a chance to work it out through self-discovery. I

REFLECTIONS ON LEADERSHIP

watch their body language for signs they are about to give up or they are about to hit a breakthrough.

If they are about to give up, I give encouragement. If they are about to make a breakthrough, I stay out of their way, then cheer them when they arrive.

I've learned this approach through trial and error and classroom learning. Too much action is micromanaging. Too little action is laissez-faire. Both are fatal to leadership.

Even when leaders appear to be doing nothing, they are doing everything.

"No one wakes up in the morning to go to work with the hope that someone will manage us. We wake up in the morning and go to work with the hope that someone will lead us."

Bob Chapman

What comes to mind when you think of a manager? It's probably not positive, and that's too bad. Managers are not necessarily a bad thing. Managers take care of the assets. They ensure staffing levels are met. They control direction. They develop strategy. They develop goals and objectives. They develop key performance indicators.

They are good at understanding numbers.

But people are not numbers.

REFLECTIONS ON LEADERSHIP

Too many organizations define success by numbers. What they miss out on is that if you take care of people, the people will take care of the numbers.

Organizations need managers, and they need leaders. Those two are not always the same, and they are not mutually exclusive. It is not common for a manager to be a good leader, but it is possible.

In 2017, *Inc.* named Bob Chapman as the third-best CEO in the world. He is the longtime CEO of Barry-Wehmiller Group. Chapman started his career as the typical business manager focused on numbers. Over time he began to see the effect this had on his people. As a father, he began to see his employees as his responsibility. He thought about how he would want a manager to treat his children once they arrived in the workforce. He believes he needs to create an environment where his employees feel safe and protected.

That's being a leader.

People don't want to be managed; objects are managed. People want to be led.

My wife owns a dog rescue, specifically for Dachshunds, aka Weiner dogs. She runs the rescue out of our home. That means I am rescuing Dachshunds too, whether I want to or not. I admit that the role has grown on me. They are a great stress reliever. I've learned as much from them as they have from me. Dogs rely heavily on body language. It's by understanding our body language that dogs have survived, even thrived as our companions around the campfire for over 14,000 years.

Studies suggest that over 55 percent of communication is through body language, yet most people are horrible at reading body language. Leaders understand communication, and leaders understand body language.

My wife specializes in the problem dogs, dogs that don't like people. The dogs that resource-guard. The dogs that are anxious. The dogs that just don't play well with others.

She has noticed a common denominator about these dogs: The owners were not leaders. When the dogs arrive at our house and discover that we are leaders, they relax. Dogs want leaders. They live in packs. They are social animals. Societies have hierarchies. People are part of their packs. If the people in their packs are not leaders, the dogs feel they need to fill the void.

At our house, there's no power vacuum. The dogs don't have to be in charge because the role of leader is already filled.

REFLECTIONS ON LEADERSHIP

We make this happen by providing structure, stability, and respect. We set rules. The dogs are fed on a schedule; they go outside on a schedule. We are predicable. They know what to expect. They trust us because we care for them, and we do not give them any reason to think that we will ever withdraw this care.

The dogs relax because we provide leadership.

People are no different. When they have a leader, they do not have to worry about where the group is headed. They can relax.

Examples abound in human beings. Watch the activity when corporations lose their leader. Specifically watch the uncertainty of stockholders. A corporation's stock can rise and fall depending on how the succession goes. People do not like uncertainly. They want to know that their corporation is in good hands. They do not want to be managed; they want to be led.

The same happens in politics. At election time, you see scrambling in the House when the party in control loses control of the House. There's politicking and positioning as the party tries to align itself around its new reality.

Stability is progress.

Action Steps

The cornerstones of leadership are trust, communication, and respect. If your employees are afraid to make a decision, they do not trust you. If they do not trust you, it's probably because you do not trust them. Trust them.

If your employees do not communicate with you, it's probably because you do not communicate with them; you issue directives. Communicate with them.

If your employees do the bare minimum for you, they do not respect you. They do not respect you because you do not respect them. Respect them. We are what we pretend to be, so we must be careful about what we pretend to be.

REFLECTIONS ON LEADERSHIP

We are what we pretend to be, so we must be careful about what we pretend to be."

Kurt Vonnegut

Vonnegut was an American writer who produced fourteen novels over his lifetime. He is best known for *Slaughterhouse-Five*. Vonnegut served in the Army during World War II; he was captured during the Battle of the Bulge and taken to Dresden. His experiences there, during the bombing of Dresden, served as the basis for *Slaughterhouse-Five*.

This quote comes from the novel, *Mother Night*, based on an American World War II double agent. As an 11-year-old, he moves with his parents to Germany. When he grows up, he becomes a Nazi, but only so that he can continue his art:

writing. He is politically apathetic. Eventually, an American agent convinces him to become a double agent

The Americans use his job as a radio personality to send coded messages. He does not understand the coded messages he sends. In his radio programs he spouts anti-Semitic propaganda. Did he believe the propaganda or was it part of his cover? Once the war ends, he remains under cover. The Americans do not want to out him as a spy. They refuse to confirm or deny that he is a spy.

The Americans help him get to New York. An American neo-Nazi group uncovers his past and threatens to expose him. He eventually ends up in an Israeli prison, held on war crimes in a jail cell next to Adolf Eichmann.

In the end, it is not very clear what the protagonist's beliefs were. Throughout the novel he is either bored or apathetic about everything. Even sitting in his cell, telling his story, it is difficult to tell how he feels about his current situation. Even if he was a spy, the anti-Semitic speech had an impact on others.

Our mind is a very adaptable organ. What we tell it enough is what it does.

REFLECTIONS ON LEADERSHIP

Many successful entrepreneurs, CEOs, and athletes advocate visualization. This is not some new-age, woo-woo activity. There is evidence that visualization works.

Soviet athletes used visualization in the 1970s. Tiger Woods has been using it since long before he was Tiger Woods. Jack Nickolas said, "I never hit a shot, not even in practice, without having a very sharp in-focus picture of it in my head."

A young Arnold Schwarzenegger imagined that his body was bigger than it currently was and that all he had to do was fill in the space. The more he did it, the more it worked. That built the confidence he needed to keep working out.

There are many studies that show that thoughts produce the same mental instructions as actions. There still may be doubters out there. If you are one of them, consider this: I am sure that you have mentally rehearsed or practiced giving presentations or having a conversation with someone. Did the real event turn out better with a little mental imagery? I'm sure it did.

To make the most of mental imagery, make the goal or image specific. Make it a vivid picture. Include sounds and smells. Think about how you want to feel at the time of the image. Make it real to you. Make your mind believe that you already have whatever that mental image is.

We all suffer those nagging negative thoughts, sometimes called monkey mind, because of the endless chatter. When you have those negative recurring thoughts, I am sure you have found that ignoring the thoughts or trying to push them aside only seems to make them more pervasive.

A technique I use it to reframe the thought. One client believed he was in a pit and could not get out. He told me that he could not stop feeling that way. I told him that when that thought that he was stuck in a pit came to him, he should follow that thought with the thought that he was building a ladder. Over time, that thought that you are stuck in the pit loses its power because you a learning that you have the ability to climb out.

Whatever it is, the reframing has to be something you believe in. If you are not excited about driving a sports car, then it does you no good to visualize yourself driving one.

Make sure you are the one experiencing the event in the visualization, not an observer. Your mind does not buy that it is you if you are watching yourself perform the practice. If you want to add more realism, write out the imagery, and I do mean write, like with a pen and paper.

The mind attaches more importance to writing that it does to typing. If you want even more enhancement, try sketchnoting, the practice of including simple drawings with your written notes. You do not have to be van Gogh or Michelangelo to make this work. Stick figures and other simple shapes are enough to make the image real in your mind.

Action Steps

I've given actionable steps above, but if you are wondering how to get started, try this.

Make yourself the hero. All of your visualization is from your point of view.

Include all of your senses. Imagine the scene completely. If you know the location, include all of sights and sounds of the area. Make the lighting bright and positive. A former coworker relayed a recent experience from the old workplace. I knew the area and people. My mind recreated the scene and it was dark, almost twilight, even though the room was a brightly lit office. My mind took a negative location and painted it dark. Use the same technique in reverse.

Write (again, on paper) out the scene. You do not have to write an award-winning book, just write 100 words about everything you want to see, hear, smell, feel, and touch.

Make sure you are the hero because, "We are what we pretend to be, so we must be careful about what we pretend to be."

REFLECTIONS ON LEADERSHIP

Do what you feel in your heart to be right, for you'll be criticized anyway."

Eleanor Roosevelt

I find it interesting that I find more notable leadership quotes from Eleanor Roosevelt than I do from her husband and former President of the United States, Franklin Roosevelt. I don't know what that says, if anything, about President Roosevelt's leadership abilities. Considering some of the agendas he pushed through, he must have had leadership skills.

Eleanor herself also had leadership skills. I know that both of the Roosevelts are controversial. Some people like them and some people hate them, and not everyone has the same opinion of both. Which is exactly what Eleanor is talking about in this quote.

If you believe in something enough, do it. Don't worry about the opinions of others. They don't pay your bills, so don't let them live in your head for free.

Olympian Jason Parker won a silver medal in speed skating for Canada. You would think that would be the highlight of his life. Most people would never have to buy a drink ever again if that were on their résumé. But for almost a decade Parker couldn't fully enjoy his medal.

Parker has talked in interviews about what happened after the Olympics. He is now a motivational speaker, but at one time he was a competitive speed skater. He competed in World Cups and World Championships. He'd missed out on three Olympics, but finally made the Olympic team in 2006.

In those Olympics, he competed in the team pursuit. As the name suggests, this is a team sport. Two teams of speed skaters are on the ice at the same time. They start on opposite sides of the ice and basically chase after each other. It's a distance race for time. Because there are so many speed skating events, and skaters have their own specialties, most countries cycle their speed skaters through preliminaries, with the best skaters competing in the medal round, but if those preliminary skaters don't do their job, the team doesn't make it to the medal rounds.

Parker skated the preliminary rounds, but did not skate in the medal round. Other skaters on the Canadian team skated in the final round and earned a silver medal. Because Parker skated the preliminary rounds, he too earned a silver medal. Again, if Parker does not do his job in the preliminary rounds, the other skaters don't even make it to the medal round.

Parker is excited, and he should be. He's finally earned an Olympic medal. He's missed the Olympics three times, and now he's finally done it. He should be happy.

One of his wife's coworkers tells her that Parker doesn't deserve the medal because he was not on the ice during the final round. Parker's wife tells Parker, and he spends the next decade feeling like he did not deserve the medal.

He will tell you that he already had some feelings of imposter syndrome and this compounded it.

Let's leave skating for a minute and look at something many Americans consider sacrosanct: the Super Bowl. When a team wins the Super Bowl, the NFL gives the team 150 rings. Granted, I am not a mathematician, but last time I checked, NFL teams had a 53-man roster. Who do the other 97 rings go to?

Well, the coaching staff usually get rings. That makes sense right? They also go to players who played on the team at some point during the season. That makes sense too, right? Some of them may go to the practice squad. Without people to practice against, the team wouldn't be any good, would they? What about the front office? Well, they may get rings too.

Is that fair? You could argue that it is. Without the front office, who pays the bills? Who maintains the facilities? Who arranges player travel?

Let's look at the Olympics again. Hockey teams are required to dress two goalies. The backup goalie may not get on the ice in the medal rounds. Does the backup still deserve a medal? He wasn't on the ice during the game. If the starting goalie is good enough, the backup goalie may not play at all during the Olympics, but he's there for every game, practice, and team meeting.

The fact is, Parker earned the medal and he deserved it, but he allowed the words of a man he didn't even know to interfere with the satisfaction and enjoyment he earned.

This man had no idea of the time and effort Parker put in. This guy wasn't with him during the early morning skate practices. He wasn't with him at restaurants and parties watching his friends drinking a beer, wishing he could have one, but did not want to ruin his training plan. This guy wasn't even with Parker in the Torino Oval Lingotto when Parker was competing.

This guy knew nothing about Parker and the path he had taken to get to the Olympics, yet he felt he was entitled to an opinion about what Parker was and wasn't entitled to.

And Parker let the guy live in his head for almost a decade.

To be clear, Parker finally evicted the guy and is now able to enjoy his accomplishments.

I am not casting stones at Jason Parker. We have all been there. We all allow people who don't have any right to judge us, to live in our head. It's happened to me and if you say it hasn't happened to you, you are not being honest with yourself.

There are many reasons people might criticize others. According to psychologists, some of the reasons include:

- They feel threatened by your competence.
- They have a controlling personality.
- They want to make you look bad to draw attention to themselves.
- They feel insecure and are over-compensating.

Some of the ways of dealing with criticism include:

- Determine if you value the person's opinion. If you don't, there's no need to listen to them.

- Don't respond immediately. Give yourself a chance to calm down and deliberately reply.

- Learn to recognize if it is constructive or destructive criticism. One is meant to help you; the other is meant to harm you. If the criticisms are about behaviors, they are probably constrictive. If they are about attitudes, they are probably destructive.

- Let it go. Is it going to matter in five minutes? How about five days or five years?

Above, in the quote from Mark Goulston, I talked about negativity bias. It rears its ugly head again. As a survival instinct, our mind focuses on the negative, so we don't make the same mistake twice. That survival instinct is based on a much different life. Today, there are not as many Saber-toothed tigers running around, not literally, anyway, although there are figuratively.

Our brain still perceives threats we face today as having the same life-and-death consequences today as they did thousands of years ago. We need to learn to deal with that constant nagging voice.

Sometimes, just knowing about the problem is enough.

REFLECTIONS ON LEADERSHIP

Action Steps

Next time you find your critic's voice in your head, acknowledge it, then respond with a more positive answer.

If your critic tells you that you are not good enough, then when you hear their voice in your head, respond by thinking, "But I am getting better." Over time, you'll notice that the voice gets quieter, until eventually it goes away.

Leaders don't inflict pain, they share pain."

Max De Pree

D e Pree was the CEO of the family business, an office furniture company, for seven years, then transitioned to the board. His book, *Leadership is an Art,* sold over 800,000 copies.

One of the key tenants of leadership is trust. Trust is a two-way street. Leaders have to trust their followers to do the work without interference. Followers have to trust leaders to take care of their emotional, and development needs. Part of sharing pain is protecting the followers and followers trusting that they can share their problems with their leader.

REFLECTIONS ON LEADERSHIP

Leaders must be willing to take on the pain of their followers. Without sharing their pain with their leaders, followers will never be able to focus on work. Followers have to know that they work in a safe environment where their leaders are not going to inflict more pain on them.

People have lives. Sometimes life brings pain. Followers have to know that their job is not going to add to that pain.

There's much ado about work/life balance. The idea is that you use your personal life to shed the stress and pain developed from your job. This is a horrible premise. It presupposes that jobs are pain, and there is no way to get around it. This gives leaders permission to inflict pain on their followers. This premise presupposes that leaders are entitled to inflict pain and stress on their followers.

I do not remember that as part of the social contract. Why do I have to agree to allow my employer to abuse me, to stress me out? If this is acceptable, then it is also acceptable that I have to give up part of my personal life to detoxify. How is that just? My personal life is my time. Why should I be expected to use my time to wash away the pain inflicted on me by my employer? If my employer inflicted the pain, shouldn't the detoxification happen on their time?

Expecting me to detoxify on my time also steals time from my family. If I go home in a foul mood because of a toxic work environment, and I need alone time to clear my mind, my family suffers. They have already given up at least eight hours that I spent away from them at work. They sent me off hoping for the best, wanting me to provide for them, but because my employer has tacit societal approval to subject me to a toxic environment, I come home from my eight hours of work worse off than I did when I left home.

Here is an idea that is much better than expecting an employee to work in a toxic environment, and expecting them to fix themselves. If organizations actually took care of their employees, protected them, shared their pain, and provided an environment where employees did not need to detoxify and distress themselves, then there would be no need for a work/life balance.

Action Steps

First, you have to find out if you are a toxic boss. Here are some common signs. Answer the questions honestly.

Is coaching employees a chore? Leaders enjoy coaching people. Leaders feel responsible for their followers' career advancement. Coaching is part of that advancement.

Do you have to double-check the work of your followers? I've said many times that trust is a pillar of leadership.

REFLECTIONS ON LEADERSHIP

Granted, you are responsible for your followers' work, but are you checking every little detail? Do you create triple, quadruple, and quintuple check systems? That's going far beyond checking their work; that's a lack of trust and a sign of insecurity.

Do you know at least one personal thing about each follower? If you do not, and you have no desire to, then you are probably treating your followers like objects.

Do you gaslight your followers? Gaslighting is a form a manipulation where the perpetrator lies to their victims about their performance, actions, or behaviors to get the victims to question themselves. One particularly toxic manager I knew often lied to their followers about their skills and abilities in an attempt to motivate them. If this is your favorite managerial technique, you are a toxic boss.

If you found some uncomfortable answers, it's OK. Everyone can change; you just have to decide that you want to. If you find you need to change, follow the action steps in this book.

The growth and development of people is the highest calling of leadership."

Harvey S. Firestone

Harvey Firestone if the founder of the Firestone Tire and Rubber Company. Firestone worked for the Columbus Buggy Company, and in 1890, he formed his own company to create rubber tires for buggies. Ten years later, he saw the potential to make tires for the fledgling automotive industry. That's when he rebranded himself and formed Firestone Tire and Rubber Company.

Firestone's company grew to the point that he, Henry Ford, and Thomas Edison were the leaders of the automotive industry. They became friends and vacationed together.

REFLECTIONS ON LEADERSHIP

The Ford and Firestone families were so close that Firestone's granddaughter, Martha, married Ford's grandson.

Firestone was known to be a great businessman. Based on this quote, I expect he was also a great leader.

Leaders are teachers and mentors. They recognize that to get the most out of their followers, leaders must grow and develop staff. There are several reasons for this. If you want the team to succeed, the members always have to be moving forward. Followers must challenge themselves and grow if the leader wants the organization to grow.

One of the most effective motivation techniques is to provide followers with a chance for growth and development. Followers know that if they ever want to be a manager or leader, they must grow and develop. Leaders who actively teach followers new skills and abilities make themselves more appealing to followers.

Several quotes in these pages (including one from Henry Ford) speak to the duty, no, the requirement of great leaders to create more leaders. The ultimate goal of a leader should be to create their replacement. A team should be so skilled that they do not need the leader standing there, watching the followers do the job.

Any leader who cannot trust their followers to do the in their absence has not done a good enough job of growing and developing their staff. Unless leaders want to perform or supervise every task their followers are assigned to, leaders must invest in and value their followers.

Anything less than that and they are failing their followers.

During Firestone's lifetime, Firestone Tire and Rubber Company created a number of products that became industry standards, such as non-skid tires; a dismountable rim that allowed the wheel and the tire to be removed together, thus allowing for the spare tire; and gum-dipping, which made tires stronger. Those are only a few of the innovations Firestone Tire and Rubber Company developed during Firestone's lifetime.

If Firestone does not invest in the growth and development of his followers, then he, not they, will have to come up with all of the innovations listed above and others I did not bother to list.

Firestone Tire and Rubber Company does not become what it is without Harvey Firestone valuing and investing in his followers.

REFLECTIONS ON LEADERSHIP

Action Steps

Start by identifying the strengths of your followers. Make it a habit to identify one strength of at least one of your followers each day. Do not let your perceptions of their weaknesses factor in; only look at the strengths they bring to the team. Do not identify the same strength for the same follower more than once.

Eventually, you will find ways to assign staff to roles you know they can fill. On multiple occasions, I have assigned staff to tasks that they have excelled at. Managers later confided in me that they did not know that those staff possessed those skills. Of course they did not; they had not taken the time to look at them as anything other than a warm body.

Waste no more time arguing about what a good man should be. Be one."

Marcus Aurelius

Aurelius was known as "the philosopher" by his contemporaries. He was the last of the so-called Five Good Emperors (Nerva, Trajan, Hadrian, and Antoninus Pius are the others). He was also the last Roman Emperor of the Pax Romana, or Roman Peace.

This period of about 200 years was characterized by internal peace and stability. Do not read this to mean that this period was without war; it just means that for this time period, Rome did not suffer civil war.

Prior to this, Rome had suffered nearly 200 years of civil war. To the Romans, peace seemed to be defined not as an

REFLECTIONS ON LEADERSHIP

absence of war, but the lack any opponents who had the will or ability to continue fighting.

Throughout the Pax Romana, Rome was at war with many of its neighbors as it tried to expand its boarders.

Aurelius was a stoic philosopher. His writings, *Meditations*, are the major source of understanding about stoicism in the modern age.

Having written *Meditations* as a source for his own guidance, it is unlikely that he ever intended his writings to be published.

His writing reflects his stoic beliefs. It is plainly written and without flourish. It is written as one man to another and is easily relatable.

One thing to remember, though, is that he was writing about himself. This was his journal, so what you are reading was his inner monologue.

One of his major themes in *Meditations* is being a good man. Aurelius writes to himself about what the attributes of a good man are. He asks himself if he can consider himself a good man.

Finally, in the last third of the books (there are twelve volumes), he tells himself to stop worrying about it and just be a good man.

He's quiet on the subject for a while (until about the last quarter), then his monkey mind starts at him again and he asks himself again if he is a good man.

Here's a man who is clearly a good man. Many of his contemporaries think he is a good man, and many modern scholars agree, and he is still wrestling with his own inner doubts. The monkey mind is chattering away.

In typical stoic tradition, this is a short quote, two sentences and fourteen words, and there are two important lessons.

First, if there is something you want to do or be, do it. Don't waste time arguing about it; do it. If your team needs a leader, step up and do it.

Second, even the greatest minds and most powerful people are wracked with self-doubt. Do not let it stop you. Imposter syndrome is everywhere. Everyone feels it, including Roman emperors.

The difference is that good men and women push through it and do great things.

REFLECTIONS ON LEADERSHIP

Action Steps

Your first action step is to be a leader, no matter where you are on the corporate ladder. Your peers need leaders too.

Your second action step is to let go of those doubts. Ignore the monkey mind. This is not always easy. One technique I use is to focus on something else. My morning routine is to ride my bike trainer while watching rugby on the DVR. This is supposed to be me time, not work time. When I find myself thinking too much about work, I focus on the ball. I do nothing but watch the ball as players pass it, kick it, and scrum over it. After some practice, this quieted the monkey mind.

You can also redirect the chatter. Most of what the monkeys are talking about is negative. Reframe the chatter. If the monkeys are yelling about your perceived mistakes in your presentation, think about what you did right. Don't think about the guy who cut you off in traffic; think about the dozens of reasons he may have had to do it. Was he rushing to see his wife at the hospital? Did he get in an argument with his wife? Whatever the reason, he cut you off, so redirect the thoughts and quiet the monkeys down.

We must be silent before we can listen. We must listen before we can learn. We must learn before we can prepare. We must prepare before we can serve. We must serve before we can lead"

William Arthur Ward

Ward was a motivational speaker and writer, born in Louisiana in 1921. In 1942, he joined the U.S. Army as a private. Four years later when he left the army, he had risen to captain.

He published articles in numerous magazines and is credited as one of the most quoted people in *Quote*, a magazine for inspirational speakers.

There is a lot of knowledge in the quote, but it is very digestible.

REFLECTIONS ON LEADERSHIP

Listening is almost a lost skill. Too often, we are formulating a response before the other person has even finished speaking. We have already made our mind up about what the speaker is going to say and about what they mean.

We are problem solvers. We are ready to solve your problem. and if you would only shut up, we would tell you exactly how to solve the problem you have not even told us about yet.

Ward takes it a step further. He says we have to be silent. So I get that it is tough to listen when your mouth is open, but silent?

Yes, but he doesn't mean mouth closed and brain engaged formulating an answer. He means silent, as in quiet the chattering monkey mind that's trying to remind you that you have to get groceries tonight.

He wants you to shut everything down and prepare to listen. Stop typing on your computer. Put your phone away. Take your phone out, and turn off all notifications. Throw your phone in a drawer. Slam the drawer shut. Lock the drawer. Now, shut up and prepare to listen.

I had a supervisor who would look me in the eye while I was talking to him, and keep typing. It was so off-putting that I have worked very hard to give my followers my undivided attention.

I am very capable of the kind of cognitive shifting and task shifting required to do what my supervisor did, and I know because I have done it.

When I was working on my Master's degree, I could work on a paper, watch a movie, and talk to my wife about the movie all at the same time. It is not a question of whether I can effectively do it; it is a question about how my follower feels about me doing it.

I can tell you first-hand that as a follower, you do not feel valued when a supervisor does this kind of task shifting when you are communicating something important to you.

And don't think it's OK to have your phone out and just ignore it. Phones are designed not to be ignored. They make all sorts of sounds, vibrations and flashes to get your attention. They are like a toddler begging you to look at them.

Numerous studies have found that just the presence of your cell phone can cause the person you were talking to, to feel less connected with you.

Do your followers a favor and get rid of your phone.

REFLECTIONS ON LEADERSHIP

Listening is so key because if you don't listen, you will never learn. You should always strive to learn, especially when you are a leader. There is always a better way of doing things. Listen to your follower so you can learn about them and from them.

Your followers tell you about emergencies looming on the horizon, and you simply have to listen, really listen (shut up that monkey mind), to learn what knowledge they have to pass on to you.

If you don't care about the knowledge your followers possess, you are not a leader.

Once you have learned what your follower's needs are, only then can you prepare to solve their problem.

Your preparation has to serve your follower. Have you ever received bad advice from someone? The advice was probably bad because they were not serving you.

One of the definitions of "serve" is to "be of use in achieving or satisfying." The advice didn't work for you because the advice giver was not serving you. They were not interested in achieving or satisfying your need.

They failed to listen or learn or prepare to serve you.

Only after you have served, that is, listened to the problem, then learned how to prepare a solution that will satisfy your follower's needs, will you have been a leader.

Action Steps

Active listening is one of the most effective techniques for leaders. When your follower speaks, allow them to talk. You are taking mental notes. When they are done, summarize what they have said. The common form is to start with "What I hear you saying ...." This allows you to summarize, but you admit that it is not complete or 100 percent accurate. You also admit that it is what you heard, but maybe not what your follower said. That gives them a chance to clarify.

Now that you have listened, you can learn how to help them. You can prepare, serve, then lead.

> Leaders think and talk about the solutions. Followers think and talk about the problems."

Brian Tracy

It's easy to point out faults and failures. Anyone can point out that the sky is falling. It takes a leader to figure out a way to push the sun back up in the sky.

Leaders have to be optimistic and not focus on the problems. They need to focus on solutions. Leaders are optimists. Followers look to their leaders for some kind of guidance. Followers look to their leaders for signs about how to act and react to any situation. If leaders focus on problems, then so do the followers. If leaders focus on solutions, then so do the followers.

I have seen followers react to the way their leaders act, with both positive and negative reactions. Leaders who allow fear into their voices may not realize the impact the sound has on their followers. I have witnessed followers who, upon hearing fear creep into the voice of their leader, begin to falter.

Followers learn how to react based on how their leaders react. A leader looking for solutions teaches their followers to look for solutions. Followers who look for solutions become proactive. Proactive followers help leaders look for solutions. They become helpers. If followers know their leader wants solutions, they come to the leader with solutions, often before a problem becomes an emergency.

Leaders looking for a solution are not looking to blame. There may indeed be a person upon whom the blame lies: the leader. Everything that happens with the team is the leader's fault. If one of the team members causes a problem, the leader is at fault. Did the leader provide enough training? Did the leader provide clear guidance to the team member? Did the leader give the team member a clear vision of the project? Did the leader not recognize that the team member needed help?

Followers fear, and do not trust, a leader who is looking for blame and not solutions. Leaders who look for blame and not solutions create followers who look out for themselves. They create followers who do not form a team. They create

REFLECTIONS ON LEADERSHIP

followers who are only looking out for their own self-interests, not the interests of their team, their leader, or their organization.

Followers need leaders who look for solutions.

"Great leaders are almost always great simplifiers who can cut through argument, debate, and doubt to offer a solution everybody can understand."

Colin Powell

Einstein said that if you can't explain it simply, you don't understand it well enough. Both of these men are known for understanding complex situations, one in the field of science, the other in the austere field of combat.

Powell had to deal with hierarchy. In his world, his vision had to be filtered down through each level of the hierarchy. It's like the telephone game. If the vision is not easy to explain by the time it gets down to the field level, the vision is describing nothing Powell could have envisioned.

REFLECTIONS ON LEADERSHIP

Your brain has two jobs: to keep you alive and to conserve energy. If something is not going to keep you alive, your brain starts conserving energy. Have you ever noticed that when you are listening to a presentation that is not engaging or anything you're interested in that you start getting drowsy? Your brain has decided that the information is not going to keep you alive in some way (entertaining, useful information, etc.), and it needs to start conserving energy, so it starts the process of shutting you down.

If you cannot make your communications to your followers entertaining, then at least make them short so you keep their brain from tuning you out.

Creativity is important. I want my followers to think, and I want them to think the weird outrageous scenarios, so I listen to their scenarios and I usually ask some clarifying questions, like "how" and "what." Do not ask why, because it begs for them to come up with a conclusion. The other danger with "why" is that it is too open-ended and you may end up hearing about the follower's cousin's sister's college roommate, who knew a guy who did a thing. And your brain is going to start shutting you down.

I love the Socratic Method. Asking questions is how I learn things. Answering questions forces me to hone my thoughts. If I ask enough questions, I learn how my followers think and they come to the conclusion on their own.

What I often find with the worst-case scenario is that if you break the problem down to first principles, there is usually a simple solution, and it's probably one you have used in the past.

I have talked about first principles, the root of the thing, elsewhere in this book. Whatever the thing is, it cannot be made into smaller pieces. If Elon Musk can break rockets into aluminum and carbon fiber, you can break your scenario down into a few words you can convey to your followers.

Showing followers the first principles of the thing at issue usually ends the debate and arguments. It shows all sides that the issue is not as complex as they think it is. It shows the doubters that you have the situation well in hand and that they have been in this very situation before without realizing it.

Action Steps

Elon Musk breaks down First Principles thinking to these three steps.

Step 1: Identify and define your current assumptions.

REFLECTIONS ON LEADERSHIP

Step 2: Break down the problem into its fundamental principles.

Step 3: Create new solutions from scratch.

Sit down with something you are struggling with. Start with something small. You are not launching rockets, yet. For example, think about what is keeping you from finishing or starting college. Write down all of your perceived barriers. Your list might include not enough money, not enough time, or not smart enough.

You decide to talk the problem of not enough time. You look at what time you do have. How much time do you spend watching television, or playing video games? What can you do to reduce time spent traveling to college? Is there downtime you can spend studying?

Your solutions to these problems may include setting a timer when you sit down to play games, finding a college with an accelerated or online program; you may find time to study while on the train or bus. I typed and wrote rough drafts of my college papers on my phone, then emailed them to myself. When I found myself waiting in line or with unexpected downtime, I opened my email on my phone and started writing.

The supreme quality of leadership is integrity.."

Dwight D. Eisenhower

Leadership is about trust. If your followers don't trust you, they won't willingly follow you. Worse, they will do the bare minimum, which means more work for you, because you have to keep checking their work. You build that trust through integrity.

Your followers know if you act through integrity or through falsehood. People are far more perceptive than we often think. They know your actions are the truth. We have all seen leaders who speak one thing, but do another.

They know based on the consistency of your actions. Do you have a well-formulated ethos? Do your followers know how you will act before you do? Can they predict how you will react to any situation?

REFLECTIONS ON LEADERSHIP

Followers want consistency. Nothing creates anxiety like the unexpected. If their leader acts unexpectedly, they become anxious. There's enough anxiety in the world. Followers look to their leader for stability, and stability comes from integrity.

Integrity is a set of values that one holds dear. If you truly believe in the values, none of them will be contradictory and every one of your actions will be in accordance with those values. If you are acting according to your values, your followers will soon learn your values.

When your followers know your values, they know how you will respond and what to expect from you.

Your followers will model your behavior. Is your behavior worth following?

Action Steps

Step 1: Write down your values, ensuring that they support each other.

Step 2: Ensure that every action you take is in alignment with your values.

Step 3: Communicate your values.

Step 4: Test your actions and values. Ask if you would like your decisions if someone else applied them to you. Ask others if you are following your values.

REFLECTIONS ON LEADERSHIP

As we look ahead into the next century, leaders will be those who empower others."

Bill Gates

Everyone knows who Gates is. He's the slightly nerdy-looking guy who builds schools in Africa. And he owns some computer company. You see Gates now, and he seems very relaxed; he even jokes sometimes.

Does anyone remember the Gates of the 1990s? That Gates was trying to single-handedly build Microsoft and fend off the federal government in an antitrust lawsuit. That Gates looked haggard and tired. The Gates in the video tapes released by the government looks nothing like the Gates we see today. It's not a surprise considering what he was going through with his company.

Besides just getting through the trial, there may be another reason Gates is more relaxed today. Gates admits that early in building Microsoft he had trouble delegating. He was very much in charge and wanted to have control over everything.

As he grew and his company grew, Gates learned that he could not control everything, no matter how hard he tried. He tried micromanaging his programmers by editing and reviewing all of their code. He realized that was not sustainable, so he learned that he had to let some things go.

One rule of thumb to use when determining if someone is ready for delegation is to ask yourself if they can do the job 70 percent as well as you can. When they reach that threshold, then turn the task over to them. You will be surprised at how quickly they reach and even pass your skill level.

Delegating your strengths can be difficult. Delegating your weakness should be easy. We are always told to work on our weaknesses, and I agree that we should make some strides to improve areas that give us challenges. But the real solution to my weaknesses is to delegate them to someone for whom they are a strength.

It was much easier for Gates to delegate one of his weaknesses: people management. Gates knew that he was not good at managing people, so he hired Steve Ballmer to be CEO.

Gates knew that for his company to grow, he had to get out of the way and trust people. This is not an easy thing for some people to do, especially perfectionists, who are often actually insecure. Procrastinators masquerade as desiring perfection, when what they are really afraid of is imposter syndrome.

Everyone has imposter syndrome. No one is concerned about your imposter syndrome, because they are worried about their own.

When Gates talks about empowering others, a big part of that empowerment is delegation. When you delegate to followers, you are showing them that you trust them. When they do a good job, thank them.

Empowering them means that you are giving them some of your power and authority. Empowering them means you are creating future leaders.

Be a leader. Delegate to your followers.

Don't tell people how to do things. Tell them what to do and let them surprise you with their results."

George S. Patton Jr.

Telling people how to do things is the first step to micromanagement. Just providing instruction does not make you a micromanager, but at some point you have to trust your staff. Just because they don't solve the problem the way you do doesn't mean they are doing it wrong.

One of the best tools of a leader is delegation. When you delegate a task, you are trusting that person to solve the problem in their own way. You may provide some advice, but the point of delegation is to take something off your plate. If you are going to take the time to talk them through the solution, then you are not saving yourself any time.

In delegating tasks to others, I have often been pleasantly surprised with their results. Sometimes their solution is better than mine. Or, combined with mine, it could be a much better solution.

As a leader, you can also determine how well they have developed their skills. Failing miserably is still a result and an opportunity for instruction and improvement. Look for ways to allow staff to develop their skills. If they fail, but you offer encouragement, they learn to trust you.

When you delegate and they succeed, you build their confidence. This boost in confidence will help them improve.

One of the benefits of the 70 percent rule is that eventually, with your guidance and practice, your follower may be able to do the job better than you. But remember, you have to give the task over to them fully. Do not sit next to them coaching them along. That's not delegating; that's micromanaging. If the goal is to build their skill and to free up your time, what benefit is there in telling them how to do it?

Handing the task over shows them that you trust their skills and judgment. Spoon-feeding them the answers shows them you do not trust them.

Your goal as a leader is to build trust, build new leaders, and to free up your time so you can do more.

A good leader inspires people to have confidence in the leader, a great leader inspires people to have confidence in themselves.

REFLECTIONS ON LEADERSHIP

"A good leader inspires people to have confidence in the leader, a great leader inspires people to have confidence in themselves."

Eleanor Roosevelt

Here's another quote from Eleanor that makes you think she was a great leader, even if you did not agree with her politics.

Your followers have to believe in you. They have to believe you can help them reach their goal, although it's even better if they have the confidence in themselves. With confidence in themselves, your job as a leader is easier. You will still need to be there, and you will still have to coach, but you will not have to prod. Their confidence will give them motivation to go forward, and you can simply guide while they do.

You can instill confidence in your followers by providing them with encouragement. Let them know that they do a good job. Be specific. Praise is fine, but it is of little value for building confidence. Give them specifics. Tell them what they did that was praise-worthy. Do this in a timely manner. It is not enough to tell them they did a good job on the thing three weeks ago; tell them they did a good job on the thing quickly.

Give them stretch projects, projects that are just outside the reach of their skills and abilities. They will have to grow some, but this project is not so far out of their wheel-house that they have no hope of reaching it. They should have confidence that they can reach it, and reaching it will boost that confidence even more.

Seek their advice. If it's good advice, take it. If it is not good advice, explain why you cannot use the advice, but thank them for their well-thought-out advice. If you make a habit of not using their advice, though, you run the risk of becoming known as an askhole: someone who bothers others for advice, but never follows through with it.

Ask your followers their goals, then provide them the help they need to achieve them. It is important that they do the work on their own, but give them the opportunity if you can. Help them create a plan to reach the goal.

REFLECTIONS ON LEADERSHIP

Listen to them. This should actually read "hear them." We listen to things all of the time; hearing is something else. If someone tells you a story or anecdote, chances are there is a message behind it. They may be trying to tell you something. Direct communication is not always easy, especially from follower to leader. They may not have the confidence to tell you something directly, but they can tell you through a story, if you will only listen. Role authority means that they look at your relationship differently than you do.

You can build that confidence if you hear what they are saying and show them that you understand. They may reveal the root cause of an issue that is bothering them. If you can help with the resolution of that trouble, you can built trust. Building trust increases their confidence in you, which leads to building confidence in themselves.

And that is what makes you a great leader.

Action Steps

We often tell leaders to provide feedback to their followers. We do not often tell leaders what feedback looks like. Fortunately, there is a script you can follow to deliver both positive and negative feedback. I have seen this script in many formats; I have even used it myself for years before I saw it in print.

Deliver both in the same tone of voice. Deliver both as close to the action as possible. Unless the behavior continues, never mention the negative event again.

The script is simple. Ask if you can give feedback. Describe the behavior. Describe the impact of the behavior. Ask the follower how they will continue or correct the behavior. Summarize what they say.

That's it.

Positive:

"Bob, can I provide some feedback? When you follow the meeting agenda, it helps keep the meeting on track. What can you do to keep doing that?"

"I guess I can ask all of the attendees what they need to talk about, and send the agenda out beforehand."

"So, you will ask for input, and send out the agenda. Thanks."

Negative:

"Bob, can I provide some feedback? When you do not follow the meeting agenda, the meeting goes off track and makes the meeting far less productive. What can you do to correct that?"

"I guess I will be more assertive about reminding people to stay topic and not engage in sidebar conversations."

"So, you will be more assertive about the agenda and sidebar conversations. Thanks."

The ultimate measure of a man is not where he stands in moments of comfort and convenience, but where he stands at times of challenge and controversy."

Martin Luther King, Jr

If anyone knows what it is like to stand in times of challenge and controversy, it is Martin Luther King, Jr. I cannot begin to describe the depression and humility he suffered during his life. As a young boy, be befriended a white child. The friendship continued until the two went to school. King and the boy had to go to two different schools. Soon after, the white boy's father would not allow them to be friends anymore.

When he was 12, King blamed himself for the death of his grandmother, and he jumped out of a second-story window.

REFLECTIONS ON LEADERSHIP

According to King, his father repeatedly whipped him until he was 15. During much of his early life, King questioned Christianity and suffered from depression.

Despite being a Black man growing up in the segregated South, and despite his upbringing and self-doubt, King became a leader of a peaceful civil rights movement. Considering his background and the spying on him by his own government, it is easy to imagine that King could have turned out to be militant.

Where he stood in times of challenge and controversy spoke volumes about King. To be a great leader, you need to stand up in times of challenge and controversy. You do not have to change the world, but you can change the lives of your team.

Your goal should always be to make life better for your team. You need to stand up for your team. Of course, that does not mean dying on every hill, and winning battles at the cost of the war.

King faced just such a possibility when he went to Chicago. He discovered that some of his protests could lead to violence, so he worked out a deal with Mayor Daley to avoid possible violence.

King did not stop his marches; he chose to be tactical about them. King wanted to avoid violence because he knew that would cause even more resistance to the civil rights movement. He wanted to be the face of a peaceful movement. If his marches resulted in violence, even violence started by others, he could not make that claim.

King stood up for what he believed in the face of controversy and challenge, but he did it tactically. He did it in a way that he could win the war, if not the battle. I am not here to argue that the movement that King advanced has achieved its goals, but I think I can safely say that the movement is further along today because of where he stood in times of challenge, and controversy.

REFLECTIONS ON LEADERSHIP

Nearly all men can stand adversity, but if you want to test a man's character, give him power."

Abraham Lincoln

L incoln would be on anyone's list of best presidents. If power tests character, Lincoln passed that test, however you feel about the Civil War or his navigation of the politics. He was charged with holding a fragile new nation together.

During the war, he remained humble. He enjoyed nothing more than visiting the troops. He even compared heights with the tallest soldiers in the camps. It is hard to imagine any recent president standing back-to-back with a soldier to compare heights.

Lincoln's most famous speech, the Gettysburg Address, is only 271 words. Lincoln took the stage after Edward Everett's two-hour oration. Lincoln could have used the event to talk about himself; instead, he turned to the task at hand. They were there to dedicate the Soldiers' National Cemetery on the grounds of the Gettysburg battlefield.

Lincoln acknowledged that their speeches would not make the ground more hallowed. To Lincoln, nothing he said that day made it more hallowed. Lincoln did not think that his speech would be remembered. "The world will little note, nor long remember what we say here..." Yet it is remembered as one of the greatest speeches in American history. Say the words "Four score and seven years ago..." and people know you are talking about the Gettysburg Address.

According to Lincoln, power does not change you; it magnifies who you are. If you are a person of character, you will use your power to do the same, but you are the same person.

Lincoln was a humble, quiet man before he became president, and he was a humble, quiet president.

Action Steps

To keep your ego in check, do the following:

REFLECTIONS ON LEADERSHIP

- Write down your values. Keep it simple. Five or six words you live your life by or want to live your life by.

- Keep those values nearby. Ensure you live by them. Ensure everything you do aligns with your values.

- Ask for feedback, and mean it.

The best executive is one who has sense enough to pick good people to do what he wants done, and self-restraint enough to keep from meddling with them while they do it."

Theodore Roosevelt

President Roosevelt is known for many things. He spent his life as a leader, including roles as the New York State Assembly minority leader, Colonel in the New York State Militia, President of the New York City Board of Police Commissioners, Assistant Secretary of the Navy, Colonel of the First U.S. Volunteer Cavalry Regiment (the Rough Riders), Governor of New York, Vice President and President of the United States.

Roosevelt had many opportunities to learn and refine his leadership skills in different arenas. He would have learned

REFLECTIONS ON LEADERSHIP

how to lead in the best of environments and in the most austere environments, so when he talks about leadership, there is reason to listen.

The fact that what he said mirrors what modern leadership thought leaders are saying today is even more reason to listen.

Modern executives are taught to delegate what they can to others and to not get in their way. Meddling with those you delegate to is micromanagement. If you are not going to trust them with the job, why give it to them?

Roosevelt talks about picking good people. In teams, you want to pick people whose skill set augments your weaknesses. You can work on your weakness, you should work on your weaknesses, but they will always be your weaknesses. There's no shame in that; the only shame is in not admitting that you have weaknesses.

Think about baseball: A pitcher's weakness is probably hitting. Your pitchers will take some batting practice, especially if they are going to be in National League parks, but they are not going to spend time in the cage at the expense of their pitching workouts.

Likewise, you are not going to have your centerfielders work on infielder drills.

The solution to your weakness is finding the teammate whose strength is your weakness.

In this quote, Roosevelt also speaks about self-restraint; this can be difficult, but it is a sign of maturity. Mature people show self-restraint. For creative people this may be difficult, but that's why you have a team and systems. Creative people need to be able to express their creativity, but if you are going to be able to focus on your business and run it, you need your team to do the non-creative things and systems to guide your creativity.

Leaders know their strengths, know their weaknesses, and know when to stay out of the way.

REFLECTIONS ON LEADERSHIP

The single biggest way to impact an organization is to focus on leadership development. There is almost no limit to the potential of an organization that recruits good people, raises them up as leaders and continually develops them."

John C. Maxwell

I wrote about Maxwell earlier. He is a well-known speaker and author on leadership. Many of his writings and work are based on leadership within the church, but that does not mean that the information cannot be applied elsewhere. That is certainly true of this quote.

Leadership in a church has many of the same characteristics as leadership in a Fortune 500 company, a school, or the military. The leadership may be aiming for other missions or in other environments, but people are all the same and leadership is about people.

To get the most out of your organization, you must develop your leaders. Leadership is not just about barking orders and hoping your orders are followed; it's about building trust in your followers. Trust goes both ways; if they do not feel that you trust them, they will not trust you.

Leaders must also learn about developing emotional intelligence, which is little more than learning to identify emotions in others and yourself. In short, developing empathy.

To many, emotional intelligence may seem like touchy-feely stuff that you do not have time for. Believe me, I am right there with you; I have long disregarded emotions. However, learning to identify them in others gives me a clue to what frame of mind they are in. Are they in the right frame of mind to complete tasks and projects I assign to them? Sometimes getting followers in the right frame of mind to complete tasks is as easy as finding out what is wrong.

The added benefit to improving my emotional intelligence is that I can identify my feelings and the impact they are having on me. Once you recognize that an emotion is working on you, you can work on figuring out the root cause and work on a solution.

REFLECTIONS ON LEADERSHIP

Since I have been working on my own emotional intelligence, I do not know what overall effect it has had on me, but my followers seem to trust and respect me more. I feel that I am getting more out of them.

The point here is that there is always more to learn about leadership. I have taken it upon myself to develop leadership skills. In one of the organizations I have worked for, there was little emphasis on leadership development. First-time supervisors are sent to a one-week class and given some tools, but the training is never followed up on. There is no work done to ensure that the new leader is even using the tools, let alone how effectively.

The organization also feels that the skills and abilities for one level of leadership are the same at all levels of leadership. That's simply not true. First-level managers supervise staff in day-to-day operations, and they have to accept that they are no longer doing the job. They are making sure the job is getting done and done effectively. Their bosses are managers of managers, who have to look at a slightly larger picture and have to accept that they are no longer managing the first-line followers. They are farther away from the work. They have to trust that their followers are getting the most out of their followers. They have to trust that training is occurring. They also have to coach and mentor those they manage and prepare them to take the manager of manager job in the future.

The manager of manager's boss is the manager of functional areas. Their view is getting even broader. They are even further away from the work, but have to trust that everyone below them is doing their job.

This progression goes on. One of the causes for poor leadership is the manager's inability to let go of the work they did at the previous level of management. There is a great temptation to reach down a level, sometimes more than one, and direct actions of those below them. This is micromanaging, and leadership-wise, there almost nothing more destructive than that.

Micromanaging is the ultimate sign that managers do not trust their followers. If you want your followers to stop working for you, start by telling them how to do everything.

If managers do not receive training and coaching at every level of management, they never grow and develop the skills they need to be effective leaders.

When people tell me that they do not need training because they have twenty years of experience, I ask if they have twenty years of experience or one year of experience twenty times.

REFLECTIONS ON LEADERSHIP

Continue to train and develop your staff so you do not have an organization filled with staff who have multiples of one year of experience.

Action Steps

Even if your corporation does not offer leadership training, you can work on your own. The "knowing-doing gap" is well known. Reading a book about something is little good if you do not know the steps to take to implement the theory.

I have given you action steps in here to help your followers bridge the gap. Now, apply them to yourself. Look at what you want to do, say improve communication with your followers. Start with something small, like giving positive feedback (giving positive feedback is easier than giving negative feedback). Set a goal of giving positive feedback to someone once a day for a month. When you are comfortable with the process, then flip the script and practice with negative feedback.

When you are comfortable with that, look at your goal: improve communication. Your next objective then could be to improve your one-to-ones.

By so doing, soon, you will have bridged the communication "knowing-doing gap."

Don't find fault, find a remedy."

Henry Ford

Anyone can find fault. It takes zero talent to find fault. On Monday mornings across America, you can find millions of people who spent all day Sunday sitting on the couch who are finding fault with the actions of skilled millionaires.

Finding fault is easy and generally unproductive. Plus, people who specialize in finding fault are exhausting. No one wants to spend time with a know-it-all who is always pointing out what you have done wrong. These people drain your mental energy and leave you feeling like you can do nothing right. Where's the reward in spending time with people like that? Unfortunately, too many leaders have finding fault as their default setting, and their followers (and organization) suffer for it.

Instead of finding fault, focus on the solution. Figure out how to make things better by finding solutions.

One way to develop this skill is to focus on first principles. This is how Elon Musk seeks remedies to building rockets far cheaper than NASA. Musk is certainly not the first person to use this method of thinking; it has been used by the likes of Aristotle, Kant, Descartes, and Carl Sagan, but Musk has made it popular.

First principles thinking is used in many disciplines and science, including physics; that's how Musk comes by the thought process. He's famously described how when he first wanted to create a space company, he was shopping around for rockets. At $65 million, readymade rockets were a little spendy, even for a billionaire like Musk.

Musk looked at the materials to make a rocket (steel, aluminum, carbon fiber) and found that the materials are far less expensive than the rocket. He reasoned that he could buy the materials and build rockets for far less than the $65 million price tag.

To use first principles, break a problem down to small parts like Musk did with his rocket and look at what you can create from that situation. Military strategist John Boyd offers a thought experiment. Think about a motorboat with a skier behind it, a military tank, and a bicycle. Break these items down and you have an engine, a hull, and skis; treads, armor plates and a gun; handlebars, wheels, gears, and a seat. Now what can you make from these?

The common solution is a snowmobile. If we are going to use this training, we have to go beyond the previous solutions. What about an amphibious motorcycle using the hull, the bike, and the engine?

What if we take the bike chain and gears, the engine, the steel plates, the wheel guides, the tank treads, and the seats from the tank: Could we make a basic chain-drive car? We could call it the Model T. You know, "T" for tank.

Somehow, I get the nagging feeling that has already been done.

Action Steps

Look at a problem in your life. Don't make it anything big. Don't limit yourself to work. Find a problem in your personal life that needs solving, but remember to make it easy on yourself. Pick a small problem.

REFLECTIONS ON LEADERSHIP

Once you have your problem, apply the first principles theory to it. Really drill down. Break the problem down to the smallest possible elements. Only once you have done that, build a solution.

If you want to build a ship, don't drum up the men to gather wood, divide the work, and give orders. Instead, teach them to yearn for the vast and endless sea."

Antoine de Saint-Exupéry

Saint-Exupéry is known as the author of *The Little Prince*, but he was also an aviator. He spent the last years of his life trying to raise support for the liberation of France.

In the quote, Saint-Exupéry is speaking about vision and how leaders use it to motivate their followers. If you can teach your followers to enjoy the sea and instill in them the desire to see what is beyond the horizon, your followers will want to build a boat without being told to build a boat. You

REFLECTIONS ON LEADERSHIP

will not have to direct their actions; they will seek out work to accomplish the vision.

A leader's vision has to be big ideas. Big ideas get people excited. Think about Martin Luther King's "I Have a Dream" or President Kennedy's space program speech "We choose to go to the moon ... not because it is easy, but because it is hard." These speeches asked listeners to imagine a world that did not yet exist, but was within reach; they changed how a generation thought, and drove people to want change.

Your vision has to be real to you. It has to be something you are passionate about. If you are not passionate about your vision, how will you ever convince your followers that they should be passionate about it?

Don't just tell your followers about the sea; tell them about the smell. Tell them about feeling the wind in your face and the feeling of freedom being on the waves and not constrained by terrestrial concerns. Tell them what wonders they will find on the other side of the sea. Tell them about whales and dolphins, about finding undiscovered lands.

Paint your vision correctly and your followers will be organizing themselves. They will be asking, "Can we leave yet?"

Give them the vision, and once they are excited about it, make it their vision by allowing them to make the plans.

Action Steps

Write down everything you feel about your organization. Write down what drives you. Write down why you do it. Look for the themes. There will likely be two or three themes running through all that you have written.

What are your stories around those themes? What are the memories that have kept you going through your journey? Write the stories down. Include every detail you remember. Bring them to life. Edit them mercilessly. They should long enough that they convey your themes, but short enough that they can be remembered. Practice telling your stories. You should be able to tell them by memory but not sound scripted.

Now, go tell your stories.

REFLECTIONS ON LEADERSHIP

A person who is worthy of being a leader wants power not for himself, but in order to be of service."

Sam J. Ervin, Jr.

Once again, here appears a quote from a somewhat controversial figure. As with all of these figures, context is important. Ervin was no doubt an interesting figure.

Ervin was born in 1896 in Morgantown, North Carolina. He saw combat in France during World War I. He entered Harvard law School in 1917, was admitted to the bar in 1919, and completed law school in 1922. He liked to say that he attended law school backward, taking third-year classes in his first year, his second-year classes his second year, and his first-year classes in his third year. He called himself a "simple country lawyer." (Ervin's phrase became so popular that parodies of his phrase appear in many movies and television shows.)

In 1922 he won election to the North Carolina House of Representatives as a Democrat. He won reelection in 1924 and 1930. In the late 1930s and early 1940s, he served as a state judge.

He was serving as an associate justice of the North Carolina Supreme Court when Governor Umstead appointed him to fill the U.S. Senate seat vacated by Clyde Hoey. Umstead settled on Ervin because another contender advocated that North Carolina support Brown vs. Board of Education. What impact this had on Ervin's future decisions is unknown.

During his career, Ervin seemed to be of two minds on many matters. I am not going to defend any of his actions, but again context is everything. And remember, all human beings are subject to some form of cognitive dissonance that even the smartest of us fall victim to.

Ervin opposed most civil rights legislation and rulings, such as Brown vs. Board of Education, and the Equal Rights Amendment, but he was a supporter of civil liberties, such as being opposed to "no knock" search laws, and viewing data banks, and lie detectors as an invasion of privacy. Ervin even opposed President Johnson's (a Democrat) data bank privacy issues. Ervin said that this dichotomy rose from a strict interpretation of The Constitution.

Ervin's Senate career was bookended by his role in bringing down two powerful Republican opponents, Senator McCarthy in 1954 and President Nixon 1974. Ironically, in 1954 it was then-Vice President Nixon who appointed Ervin to the committee formed to determine if the Senate should censure McCarthy. Nearly twenty years later, Nixon resigned as President in the face of the findings of the Select Committee on Presidential Campaign Activities, chaired by Ervin.

I am not sure how to view Ervin or even how Democrats should view Ervin. (In the interests of full disclosure, rarely do I wholly agree with the platforms of either major party.) I think it is also important to note that one man's terrorist is another man's freedom fighter. To the United States, George Washington was a hero; to contemporary Britons, he was a terrorist, subject to hanging if caught.

Regardless of his history, Ervin knew a thing or two about leadership, as evidenced by how he was able to push through his agenda (whatever it was), and by the quote above.

Real leaders do not do what they do to consolidate their power. Their interest is in making things better for their followers. Any power a leader gains, they give to their followers.

One example of how Ervin lived out his quote is when he was appointed to chair the Select Committee on Presidential Campaign Activities. Ervin had already decided that he was not going to run for reelection to the Senate or to run for President, even though he was well respected by both major parties. He also felt a duty to try to protect The Constitution. He felt that if the accusations were true, the event would prove to be a Constitutional crisis.

A politician focused on power would have wanted to lead this committee simply because this committee could make a politician's career, the sort of career to launch a run for the Presidency or other high-level political office or as a lobbyist or an ambassadorship.

Ervin knew his political career was coming to an end, so he did not accept the chairmanship for the power. And true to his word, Ervin retired before the end of his term and went home to Morganton, where he wrote books and appeared in a few television commercials.

During his lifetime, Ervin had many opportunities (more than are listed here) to use his power for personal gain, and yet he seemed to be most happy when he played the role of simple country lawyer.

REFLECTIONS ON LEADERSHIP

Action Steps

Write down five times when you could have used your power for some personal gain, but gave it to someone else. These don't have to be big events. For example, at one time, I was the equipment manager and squad leader on a tactical team. Everyone on the team had better equipment than I did.

If you are finding it hard to come up with five examples of when you used your power to be of service, start looking for those opportunities.

"A competent leader can get efficient service from poor troops, while on the contrary, an incapable leader can demoralize the best of troops."

General John J. Pershing

General John "Black Jack" Pershing is not without his detractors, but whatever his critics may say, Pershing was formidable. He was the first American general to be given the title General of the Armies during his lifetime. (George Washington, the only other recipient of this rank, received it posthumously in 1979.) To put this in perspective, Pershing would have ranked higher than a five-star General of the Army during World War II; he would have outranked Eisenhower.

REFLECTIONS ON LEADERSHIP

Pershing led the American Expeditionary Forces in World War I. He also mentored future World War II generals George Marshal, Dwight Eisenhower, Omar Bradley, George Patton, and Douglas MacArthur.

As a cadet at West Point, he showed early promise as a leader, including as the commander of the honor guard who saluted the funeral train of General Ulysses S. Grant as the train passed West Point.

According to Pershing, a competent leader brings people up. They empower them and make them better than even they thought possible.

Incapable leaders do the opposite. They hold their people down; worse, they drive them down. The demoralize followers and sap their energy. They make their followers less than what they are on their own.

In Pershing's view, incapable leaders break down unit cohesion. This happens when troops do not trust each other or their leader. The troops form silos and do not work together. Military units rely on a troop's willingness to give their lives for one another. In Pershing's worst-case scenario, this bond no longer exists.

They are so demoralized that they no longer function as a family, as a single unit. They are now a band of single actors. This is bad in any team.

In the military, this is lethal.

Action Steps

Are there silos in your team? Is there a lack of trust? Do you trust your followers? Do your backup procedures to your backup procedures have backup procedures? Is morale low?

It's easy to blame followers, but according to Black Jack Pershing, you should look at yourself first.

REFLECTIONS ON LEADERSHIP

It is necessary for us to learn from others' mistakes. You will not live long enough to make them all yourself."

Admiral Hyman G. Rickover

Admiral Rickover is often called the "Father of the Nuclear Navy." Rickover served in the U.S. Navy for 63 years, nearly 30 of those years as an admiral. Rickover is most well- known for transitioning the Navy from diesel to nuclear power. Rickover often ruffled feathers; he apparently saw himself as the rebel later described by General Colin Powell. He had been passed over twice for promotion to admiral. He might never have received the promotion if not for the intervention of the Secretary of the Navy, Congress, and the President. Rickover's personality may have ultimately led to his forced retirement.

Mistakes are one of our greatest teachers; we have to be wise enough to learn from those we make and those that others make. The important step here is to not dwell on the mistake, because that could trigger procrastination and perfectionism. It may also trigger negative feelings that make the problem worse. Our negativity bias makes us focus on the negative. If you continue to feed into the bias, it may be difficult to pull yourself out.

Recognize the mistake, analyze the mistake in terms of first principles, and look for what you can learn from them, but do not dwell on the fact that you made a mistake. Reframe the incident as a learning opportunity, which it is.

There is also freedom in admitting the mistake. Once you take responsibility for the mistake, you are the one responsible for the solution, thus making solving the problem easier.

Unfortunately for us, we will never live long enough to make all of the mistakes that we need to learn from. This is the beauty of learning from the mistakes of others.

If you are one of those people who have to learn by doing, you could be in for a tough life. That's a stance I have never understood. I have never shot myself in the leg with a gun, but based on the mistakes of others, I never felt compelled to "learn on my own" and send a round into my leg.

This might seem like an extreme example, but it holds up, and it simplifies the argument against having to learn the lesson for yourself.

The best mistakes to learn from do not always happen right in front of us. Fortunately, the people we want to learn mistakes from tell us about their failures and successes. They do this in the form of autobiographies, podcasts, and television shows.

Great leaders, entrepreneurs, and business leaders all tell us about how they got to where they are, including the failures and successes. They want us to learn from their failures, so we can succeed.

By listening, reading, and learning about the mistakes of others, we can learn from many lifetimes, not just our own.

Action Steps

Look at a problem from the past where someone had warned you about the consequences and you did not listen to their advice.

- How did you come to the decision not to listen to the advice?
- What about the advice made you not take it?
- What steps could you have taken to make another decision?
- What did you learn?
- Would you make the same choice again?

REFLECTIONS ON LEADERSHIP

The boss drives people; the leader coaches them. The boss depends on authority; the leader on good will. The boss inspires fear; the leader inspires enthusiasm. The boss says I; the leader says WE. The boss fixes the blame for the breakdown; the leader fixes the breakdown. The boss says GO; the leader says Let's GO!"

Harry Gordon Selfridge

Many Americans will not recognize the name Selfridge. He was born in Wisconsin in 1858, and he worked several jobs until he landed a job at Marshall Field's in Chicago. The jobs showed his willingness to work and an entrepreneurial spirit. At the age of 23, he used his earnings from working in a dry goods store to start a boys' monthly magazine. He supported the magazine by selling advertising.

He worked at Marshal Field's for 25 years, rising through the ranks until he became a partner. If you have ever been annoyed at those countdown to the days until Christmas signs in department stores, you have Selfridge to thank. He was the first person to promote department store sales with that line.

In 1904, Selfridge opened his own department store called Harry G. Selfridge and Co. He sold it after two months, turning a profit.

He tried retirement, but it did not fit well with him. In 1906, he travelled with his wife to London, which had many amenities of a big city with plenty of stores and shops. What it lacked was a department store like Marshal Field's. Like any entrepreneur, Selfridge recognized a niche in the market when he saw one.

He opened his own store there, Selfridges & Co., in 1908. A careful viewer of the 2017 movie *Wonder Woman* will notice that Diana Prince goes shopping in a Selfridges & Co.

He remained chairman of the company until he retired again in 1941. He died in 1947 at the age of 89. There are still four Selfridges & Co. stores in the UK.

REFLECTIONS ON LEADERSHIP

A man this successful probably knew a thing or two about leadership, especially considering that he created a culture that allowed a store to remain open for 111 years so far.

His quote compares and contrasts bosses and leaders. According to Selfridge, bosses have many negative attributes: They drive people, they are authoritarians, they rule by fear, they are "I-centered," they lay blame, and they send you into battle while they stay behind.

Leaders, according to Selfridge, have more positive attributes: They coach, they use good will, they inspire enthusiasm, they are "we-centered," they are fixers, and they lead into battle.

Selfridge, a self-made business man from 111 years ago, has successfully tapped into all the keys of modern leadership theory. Successful leadership skills have not changed even since before Selfridge opened his stores, yet somehow his words seem new to us.

What has happened to our business culture, indeed our culture, that treating people fairly and appropriately seems like a novel concept? I am not sure I have the answer to that, but the fact that a whole generation of thought leaders who say the same thing as Selfridge said has become popular tells me that we took a turn at some point. Fortunately, we seem to be correcting.

To be fair, cultural mores are cyclical, just as business mores are be. I'm not an anthropologist, so I will not go on a dissertation about cultural changes.

I will say that a good idea is a good idea, and Selfridge was on to something here.

REFLECTIONS ON LEADERSHIP

Failing organizations are usually over-managed and under-led."

Warren G. Bennis

Bennis was the author of more than 30 books on management and leadership. He joined the U.S. Army in 1943, and he enrolled in Antioch College in 1947. He graduated with his BA in 1951, and in 1955, he earned his Ph.D. from MIT in Social Sciences and Economics. He spent much of his life in academia, but that is not to diminish his impact.

During his career, many business magazines heralded his praises. This quote gives an indication why.

As with other quotes, we see a distinct difference between leadership and management. Management is not a bad thing, but remember: Management is about numbers, while leadership is about people.

People will not care about your bottom line if you do not care about them. People need to feel that they are important. People need to feel that you care. If they do not feel that, they are not going to work hard for you.

I know of one over-managed organization whose only concern was how they appeared in internal audits, so the organization managed how employees wrote reports. They managed how well employees conducted safety and security inspections. They managed how well employees could recite policy. What they ended up with was a facility that performed well on audits.

What the management could not figure out was why employee engagement dropped year after year. Positive responses to the question of if the organization was a good place to work dropped ten percentage points in one year. Positive responses to that question dropped even further the next year.

Yet somehow the organization failed to notice that the drop in employee engagement had anything to do with over-managing and under-leading. The organization continued to promote managers and pass up leaders because the organization focused on the numbers, not the people; the organization paid the price.

Action Steps

Look at your processes. How many checks and balances do they have?

The A-10 Thunderbolt is a flying tank, designed for close ground support. I've seen footage of these planes with holes in the wings and parts hanging off, yet they still land. The A-10 depends on triple redundancy. Each system has a backup and that system has a backup, and that's it.

Triple redundancy is insurance when people's lives are on the line. But if your organiza-tion has more than triple redundancy for simple procedures, you are telling your staff that you do not trust them. The organization above had seven checks and balances for a simple building inspection. That did not tell their employees that the organization trusted them.

If that sounds like your organization, you are over-managing.

Wise leaders generally have wise counselors because it takes a wise person themselves to distinguish them."

Diogenes of Sinope

In researching this book, I have been uncertain how to approach Diogenes. He was another of the controversial figures who populated the leadership world, but in his case the controversy is not for the political stances he took.

He lived in Greece from 412 B.C. to 323 B.C. His father was a minter; he minted coins for a living. Well, he did, until he was caught debasing currency. In those days, coins were actually made of precious metals. Diogenes was exiled from Sinope for mixing non-precious metals into the coins he minted.

REFLECTIONS ON LEADERSHIP

Diogenes ended up in Athens, where he took up poverty as a virtue. He generally made a nuisance of himself, going so far as to interrupt Plato's lectures. Diogenes took the poverty theme to heart, living in a giant urn in the market place and living as a beggar.

One story goes that prior to debasing coins, Diogenes consulted the Oracle at Delphi to find out if he should debase the currency, so he did. After his exile, Diogenes thought that the Oracle meant he should debase the political currency, so he went to Athens. Ancient Greece was made up of independent city states, and Athens was the cultural center. As such, he was not well accepted there.

There are many tales about him, including one about arriving in Athens with a slave named Manes, but the slave escaped him. Diogenes supposedly said, "If Manes can live without Diogenes, why not Diogenes without Manes?"

Another story said that Diogenes was kidnapped by pirates and sold into slavery in Corinth. When he arrived in Corinth, he claimed his trade was governing men, so he asked to be sold to a man who needed a master. The phrase he used may have meant, "governing men" or "teaching values to people." Either quote could have passed the lips of a character like Diogenes, especially the latter one when speaking of values, and the crime for which he was initially exiled.

No one really knows what happened to him in slavery, or if he had even been sold into slavery.

As with so much about Diogenes, it is impossible to say what is true and what is not. The legend of Diogenes is of a man who did not take himself too seriously and spoke in puns that carried wisdom.

Pun or not, his quote here has wisdom. As Socrates pointed out, wise men know that they do not know everything and that even they need wise counsel from time to time. Diogenes, in his own peculiar way, is seconding Socrates. When Diogenes heckled Plato, sometimes it was to claim that Plato was corrupting Socrates' teachings. Plato himself described Diogenes as "a Socrates gone mad."

Most of what we know today of Socrates we know from Plato. If Plato makes a connection, albeit unflattering, between Diogenes and Socrates, it is reasonable to believe that Diogenes knew some of Socrates' teachings, though Diogenes was a child at the time.

It is also reasonable to believe that Diogenes learned about Socrates from someone other than Plato. He could have had similar beliefs to Socrates, though Plato would think these beliefs had gone mad.

Ultimately, mad or not, Diogenes offers good advice: Wise men seek wise counsel because it takes one to know one.

I am beginning to think that Diogenes' particular form of madness is contagious.

Action Steps

Look for wisdom among your counselors. Intelligence and knowledge are not the same as wisdom. Wisdom is the judicious application of knowledge. It's about applying lessons from one area of life to another.

There's a phrase that goes "If you are the smartest person in the room, you are in the wrong room." There's some truth to the phrase, but the speaker lacked wisdom.

Even if you are the smartest person in the room, everyone in the room knows something you don't.

Ask questions of everyone in your room. What do they know that you do not?

Great leaders are not defined by the absence of weakness, but rather by the presence of clear strengths."

John Zenger

Zenger is best known as the journalist who won a libel suit brought against him by former governor of New York, William Cosby, thus establishing the freedom of the press, in 1735.

Again we have a case of historical figures teaching us a lesson we should not be taking for granted. While freedom of the press is important, the quote above does merit respect in the leadership realm.

Followers want to know where a leader's strengths lie. They want to know that the leader has some technical skills

REFLECTIONS ON LEADERSHIP

in their area. But often technical skills are just the beginning. Leaders also have to have soft skills. They have to know how to communicate. They have to have emotional intelligence. They have to be able to identify strengths in their followers and deploy followers appropriately.

None of this is new, and these thoughts have been expressed elsewhere in this book. What separates this quote from other quotes about strengths is the first part of the quote, where he says "Great leaders are not defined by the absence of weakness…"

Zenger admits that leaders have weaknesses. It's not a novel concept. We all have weaknesses, and Zenger is saying that leaders need not hide theirs. Followers like to know that their leaders are vulnerable. Their vulnerability makes them human, and it's that humanity that makes them leaders. Followers know that they themselves are not perfect. It's admitting to, yet striving to overcome imperfections that make leaders appealing.

I am about to admit something about myself that might make me unpopular to some readers. I'm not a big fan of comic books and the movies spawned from them, with one exception: I like Batman. I do not like Superman.

Superman is a little too perfect. He's super. He has one weakness, and that weakness is not of this earth. He is so perfect that all he needs as a disguise is a pair of glasses.

On the other hand, Batman is full of human frailty. He is not super. He has many weaknesses; he makes mistakes. The thing that makes him likeable, the thing that makes him super, is the human spirit and drive to overcome his weaknesses. He is not defined by his weaknesses. He is great because his clear strength is his absolute desire to fight evil. It is his defining characteristic. It is his vision.

Not all of us are out to fight evil, though if I had a Batmobile, I might be persuaded to.

In his own way, Zenger was Batman going up against a super villain. Governor Cosby was corrupt. He ousted the Chief Justice of the colonial court and replaced him with one of his allies. New York attorneys, merchants, and other citizens started the *New York Weekly Journal* as a platform to criticize Cosby. Cosby had been appointed by the British monarchy, making him virtually untouchable by the colonists. To them, starting the newspaper was their only recourse.

The founders of the newspaper asked Zenger to be the publisher of the paper, even though as an immigrant he was not yet fluent in English. He wrote few of the critical articles. That could be perceived as a weakness.

His strength, therefore, must have been leading, and publishing a newspaper.

Eventually, Cosby had Zenger arrested for libel. Zenger spent eight months in jail, before his case finally went to trial. A colonial jury found that the articles critical of the governor in the *New York Weekly Journal* were factual and therefore were not libelous, thereby establishing the principle of freedom of the press.

All thanks to a Gotham City superhero.

Action Steps

Draft a list of your strengths and weaknesses. Be honest. Draft a list of strengths and weaknesses of your followers. Are there any weaknesses not are not cancelled out by strengths?

If there are, it's time to fix them.

Leadership is all about people. It is not about organizations. It is not about plans. It is not about strategies. It is all about people, motivating people to get the job done. You have to be people-centered."

Colin Powell

P owell appears on these pages several times. He came to national attention during Desert Shield and Desert Storm (what some people mistakenly call the first Gulf War). He was the Chairman of the Joint Chiefs of Staff during the war, but Powell'[s career stretched back to the Vietnam era.

As with his other quotes in this book, Powell is concise. He tells you what he is going to tell you. He gives some

REFLECTIONS ON LEADERSHIP

examples and details, then he tells you what he told you. He starts with telling you that leadership is about people. The he talks about organizations, plans, and strategies, then he talks about people.

Powell was a career military man, but he also has an MBA. He knows about organizations, plans, and strategies from both a military standpoint and a business standpoint, yet he tells us that leadership is not about any of those things.

I have never served in the military, but many of my good friends and coworkers are former military. They all talk have having plans and strategies. You do not have just Plan A. You do not have just a Plan B. You have Plans A through Z, and you may even have started on Plan AA. They know about organizations and organizing. They also know maintaining organizational integrity.

Businesses also talk about hierarchies, plans, and strategies. Do not even think about bringing in an investor or approaching a bank without detailed business plans, financials, and a slide deck.

So why does he talk about people when both his military side and business side scream that organizations, plans, and strategy are important? Because both his business and military sides say that none of those are important if you do not first take care of the people.

By definition, organizations cannot exist without people. You simply cannot have an organization of inanimate objects. Organizations are a collection of people doing things.

Strategies are ways to achieve goals and objectives. A machine does not carry out a strategy. It may be part of a strategy, but until Skynet becomes self-aware, people are still necessary to form strategies. The same with plans. Plans do not just manifest themselves; they require people both to formulate them and to enact them.

The common denominator in all of this is people.

Powell mentions that a leader needs to motivate people to "get the job done." Motivation, according to Powell, is the key ingredient to success. Then he says that a leader must be people-centered.

What does people-centered look like? There are several aspects. You have to let people know what you do and why you do it, which sounds a lot like strategy and plan. It's actually where strategies and plans *come from*, but it is all related. You cannot have strategies and plans if there is no "what" and "why."

REFLECTIONS ON LEADERSHIP

Here's the sneaky thing you may not be aware of: This is the first step of motivation. For your people to be motivated to work for you, they have to agree with your why. If they don't care about your why, they will only work hard enough for you to get a pay-check. If they agree with your why, they will work hard enough to help you achieve it.

People-centered also requires you to encourage your followers. Encouragement is not just rah, rah cheerleader stuff. You have to give praise, you have to give encouragement, but the praise and encouragement have to be properly timed.

Suppose you are potty-training a puppy. When the puppy goes potty outside for the first time, do you give praise when the puppy potties outside, or do you give praise ten minutes later after you have brought the puppy back inside? Of course you give the praise when the puppy is still outside.

People are not the same as a puppy, not quite. With people, the praise does not have to come at the precise moment of the good deed, but you do have to give it quickly. If you delay too long, you lessen the impact. You also have to ensure that the follower knows what they did to receive the praise.

Deliver encouragement while the follower is working on the task, preferably at a point that they are feeling they are struggling. You may even include an example of a time that they accomplished a similar task. Tie the example to a strength of the follower. People usually know what they are good at, but they like that you have noticed too.

Both praise and encouragement are types of motivation. See a pattern?

Moving on, people-centered also focuses on strengths. Remember that you can and should work on improving weaknesses, but they are not likely to ever rise to the level of a strength. Strengths are important to people-centered leadership in that you cannot set your followers up for failure. Do not assign them a task where they cannot capitalize on their strengths. Assigning them a task capitalizing on their strengths sets them up for success.

Success helps build intrinsic motivation. When followers are successful, they want to continue to be successful. They will look for more opportunities to be successful.

They are finding intrinsic motivation to work toward your why.

One of the last keys is to allow one of your followers to compensate for your weakness. Because you acknowledge

REFLECTIONS ON LEADERSHIP

that your follower can do something better than you, and that you trust them enough to do it for you, you have added to that intrinsic motivation you have been building on.

Take care of your people, and your people will take care of you.

The goal of a leader is to give no orders. Leaders are to provide direction and intent and allow others to figure out what to do and how to get there."

David Marquet

Marquet is a retired U.S. Navy captain who has become a leadership mentor. After years of hard work, he received a promotion to command his own submarine. He was determined to be the best submarine commander. He studied everything there was to know about his new ship including the crew. At the last minute, the Navy informed him that instead of the brand new ship and the brand new crew, he was being assigned to the lowest rated crew in the Navy.

REFLECTIONS ON LEADERSHIP

He decided that he was going to be the best anyway. So he took his crew out for sea trials. He was captaining the USS Santa Fe, a Los Angeles-class nuclear submarine. In the middle of the ocean, he directed the crew to power down the nuclear reactor. Without the reactor, the submarine has to run on battery power

The batteries only last so long. He wanted to put pressure on the crew to get the reactor restarted before the batteries went dead, so he told his officer on deck "ahead, two-thirds." The officer on the deck repeated the order "ahead, two-thirds." Nothing happened. Marquet was confused. Was there something wrong with his ship?

He asked the helmsman what was wrong. The helmsman told his captain that this ship did not have a two-thirds setting for battery power. Now Marquet was really confused. He asked the officer on the deck if he knew the ship did not have a two-thirds setting. The officer admitted that he knew that the ship did not have a two-thirds setting.

Marquet realized that the crew only knew how to blindly follow orders, even orders that did not make sense. The crew had no capacity to question orders they knew made no sense.

Any rebel that Colin Powell spoke about in a previous quote had been wrung out of this crew. They were afraid to tell the emperor he had no clothes. Marquet realized that this system was not sustainable. The captain cannot think for his entire ship.

I am on an incident management team (IMT), which are called in to help manage emergencies, such a flooding and forest fires. These teams follow management frameworks adopted by FEMA. One of the frameworks states that a leader's span of control (how many people they supervise) shall be between three and seven with an optimum of five. Retired SEAL commander Jocko Willick says that in combat, the most a leader can manage is three.

Whatever combination of training and common sense Marquet possessed, he knew that his crew of about 150 was far too many people for him to try to supervise in normal conditions. In combat, the ship would be in serious trouble.

He decided to try an approach where he told the crew his intent, and the crew was responsible for carrying out that intent. He wanted to empower his crew; he wanted his crew to be leaders, not followers, so he stopped giving orders. He expected his crew to tell him what they were going to do, and he would approve the action.

In this plan, Marquet would tell his crew that he wanted to go somewhere under battery power. His crew would respond with some speed and direction they could go.

REFLECTIONS ON LEADERSHIP

The effect was dramatic. When he took over, the Santa Fe was the worst in the fleet. Soon the Santa Fe had achieved the highest operational standing in the Navy. All other crew metrics that you care to measure improved also. Enlisted crew who chose to reenlist went up. The number of officers who went on to command their own ships went up. In all ways, Marquet was a success, because he trusted his crew.

We have talked about this idea in other parts of this book. We looked at leaders who tell their followers their vision and allow them to plan the way to the vision.

It may interest you to know that another military leader used this philosophy: the Supreme Allied Commander, General Eisenhower.

During the D Day invasion, Eisenhower did not issue a single order, because all of that had already been taken care of. He spent the day moving around headquarters, tracking the progress on the maps, talking to General Montgomery and generally trying to occupy his mind, but he was done giving orders. He simply waited to see if he had done a good enough job of communicating his intent.

Whatever you call it, success comes from painting a vision for your followers, trusting them to get you there, and staying out of their way.

One of the greatest talents of all is the talent to recognize and to develop talent in others."

Colin Powell

Leaders must identify talent among their followers, if they want to get the most out of their teams. Many people give the advice that you should work on your weaknesses, which is good advice, to a point.

How often do you think professional baseball pitchers take fielding practice? Do you think outfielders ever take to the mound? How about offensive linemen in football? Do you think they ever go run patterns with the receivers? Do hockey goalies ever run passing drills?

REFLECTIONS ON LEADERSHIP

The answer to all of these is no, at least not as part of their regular training. These are skilled professionals filling a particular role on the team.

You could argue that your organization needs people to be flexible, to be able to fill several roles, and you would be right. There are utility players in baseball. Some football players play multiple positions. It is good to train employees to fill multiple roles in your organization; it expands their skills and abilities. It also gives them a broader view of the whole organization. However, you have to accept that not everyone is going to be able to work in every position.

Focusing on weaknesses will often only yield limited improvement in weak areas and may actually harm advancement in strengths, as it takes time and attention away from those areas.

Most leaders can identify strengths in their followers through performance and measurable results. Good leaders can observe talent through behaviors. Great leaders identify talents by talking to their followers.

I once discovered that one of my followers had a head for accounting, although his job had nothing to do with accounting. Given his job, there was no performance metric I could have captured that would have told me that. There were no behaviors I could observe that would tell me about this talent. I discovered it by talking to him about his goals and dreams.

While the job he was responsible for did not require accounting, it did tell me something about his analytical and computer skills, skills that at that point were going untapped.

With a simple conversation, I learned that I had a previously unknown talent among my followers. More important, I was able to demonstrate to a follower that I was genuinely interested in him as a person and I was concerned about his future.

That bit of relationship building was far more valuable to me as leader than finding out about his hidden talent.

REFLECTIONS ON LEADERSHIP

Don't let yesterday take up too much of today."

Will Rogers

Will Rogers was a political humorist in the early 1900s. He was rare in the political commentator arena in that he found humor in both political parties. Unlike today's satirists and commentators, Rogers could find humor in and poke fun at anyone of any political leanings.

He was a Democrat, but was just as likely to support a Republican. He supported Calvin Coolidge as well as Franklin Roosevelt. About Roosevelt's New Deal, he said, "Lord, the money we do spend on government and it's not one bit better than the government we got for one-third the money twenty years ago."

DENNIS MOSSBURG

In 1928 he ran for president in a mock campaign, running as a member of the Anti-Bunk Party. During the campaign, when asked about what a farmer needs, he said, "He needs a punch in the jaw if he believes that either of the parties cares a damn about him after the election."

He did not seem to take anything too seriously. That is in alignment with the quote above. Though his acts and comments were obviously light-hearted, they hid a serious truth. He tried to reach people through humor. He did not dwell on the past and did not see any reason to.

What is not mentioned in this quote is tomorrow. My guess is that he would not let tomorrow take up too much of today either.

Without putting too many words in his mouth, I would say the Rogers is talking about mindfulness. Focus on now. You cannot change yesterday and tomorrow is not here yet. Do what you can in the here and now. Appreciate what you have, and enjoy it.

Learn what you can from yesterday, but move on.

He uses the words "take up." Yesterday is taking from today. It is stealing from today. If you dwell on the past, not only did it have a negative impact on you then, but it is robbing you now. It continues to take from you, even though you cannot do anything about it. The biggest problem is that often we think yesterday had a negative impact on us. We dwell on what we said or didn't say. We analyze and over-interpret minutia. We overthink what we think people think of us.

In reality, they are overthinking, what they think we think of them.

Your day begins as a clean slate. How you wake up (if you are not careful) impacts the rest of your day.

I am not a morning person. When I wake up, it is not all sunshine and rainbows. I take some time to build up momentum. I do not spring out of bed and have cartoon forest animals spring around the room with me as I make my bed.

That does not mean that I am in a bad mood or that I am miserable; it is just that I am slowly spooling up as my mind gets engaged.

My wife is a morning person. She loves sunrises, and she bounds out of bed at full speed. By the time I am awake, she has been up for hours. She leaves one of our dachshunds in bed with me. He has the same opinion of mornings as I do. When I wake, he usually looks at me as if asking if we really have to do this.

Watching the expression on his face is enough to start my day off right. He gets me in the right mood. I do not ruin that mood by turning on the news. I will tell you right now that I almost never watch the news; there's too much bad stuff there. The news does not make money by making people happy. Newsrooms operate off the often-told maxim "If it bleeds, it leads" for a reason.

All of the news happened yesterday. I cannot change any of it, so I am not going to focus on it.

The same with social media. I spend very little time consuming social media. Much of it is negative, and much of it happened in the past. I am not going to allow yesterday to take from today.

When I wake up, I spend time with the dog. I think about objectives for the day, and I just spend time relaxing. I am clearing the cobwebs and looking forward to today.

I use that phrase intentionally: I am looking forward. It's a positive. I want the day to be a good one, so I think about what that will entail.

Do not get me wrong; it is not always easy, and I have not always had this mindset. Much of what I know about what leadership should look like is by working in toxic work environments. Negative examples have taught me what I do not want to be as a leader.

Living in those toxic environments have already stolen too much time and energy from me. If I want to improve my now and my future, I have to choose not to allow yesterday to take away from today.

Action Steps

Each morning, before you check your phone, think about at least one thing you are grateful for. It does not even have to be big or grand, just one thing you are grateful for.

If you cannot think of anything, then at least be grateful that you woke up.

Everything you've ever wanted is on the other side of fear."

George Addair

This is such a simple quote. It's deceptively simple. It's so simple anyone can do it. So why don't more people let go of their fear and roll the dice?

Because fear is not simple. Fear is a survival skill. Fear has kept us alive for tens of thousands of years. Fear is that quiet voice from the limbic system warning us that if we are not careful, the Saber-toothed tiger will eat us when we go to our favorite berry bush.

At last count, there weren't that many Saber-toothed tigers left, yet our limbic brain is still working hard to protect us.

So how do we overcome fear? It would be nice just to say "Get over it." The problem is that fear is often a long-held habit. We hold on to it because even if we do not like it, fear provides a structure. It is something to hold on to in the face of the unknown.

There are many different strategies for dealing with fear; here are a few that I have found success with.

We hear much about stories these days. What story do you tell your customers? What stories do customers tell you? I would argue that the important question is "What story do you tell yourself?"

When you feel that twinge of self-doubt, that inner dialogue that tells you that you aren't good enough, reframe the conversation.

Instead of "I'm not good enough," try "I'm getting better every day."

Whatever works for you, find a mantra the counters the negative inner dialogue with positive thoughts.

Have goals and a plan. Think about what you want to do, then write out a goal, but keep it short, 250 words or less. Use a pen and paper. The brain seems to have a much stronger connection to the act of writing than to the act of typing.

When you have your plan, review it often and ask yourself if you are doing something every day to bring you closer to your goal.

If you are not, then fix yourself.

Step out of your comfort zone every day. This doesn't even have to be something big, just one small thing that stretches your comfort zone.

An introvert may want to try engaging in a friendly conversation with a stranger or a nodding acquaintance.

It doesn't matter what it is; just get comfortable being a little uncomfortable and soon you will be on the other side of fear.

REFLECTIONS ON LEADERSHIP

It is absolutely necessary... for me to have persons that can think for me, as well as execute orders."

George Washington

Washington is one of those men many people know about, but few people really know. His legend has far overshadowed the man. I am not trying to take anything away from him, not in the least.

He worked on his image all his life. He was never quite satisfied with where he was. He always worked on self-improvement. His father died when George was only 11, leaving George family with limited funds for education. Young Washington was left to teach himself.

As a handwriting exercise, he copied *Bienséance de la conversation entre les hommes* (a book on etiquette) creating what he called *The Rules of Civility and Decent Behavior.* They included guidelines for behavior and courtesies, stressing the importance for humility. These 110 rules became the rules he would live by.

In terms of formal education, Washington was the least-educated of the founding fathers, but do not think that he was lacking intelligence. He studied geometry and trigonometry in preparation for his career as a surveyor.

Washington knew that his contemporaries were better educated than he was. As a result, he was self-conscious and worked hard to cover his educational deficiencies. Perhaps it is from these feelings that he gives us the quote above or perhaps the quote comes from his understanding of leadership.

Washington understood that leaders cannot do all of the thinking for his people. He chose to hire good people and stay out of their way.

Remember, this is a time long before modern communication. Before a battle, Washington has to communicate the commander's intent, then send his officers off into battle with little or no guidance from him once the shooting started.

REFLECTIONS ON LEADERSHIP

In an age when most communication was only as fast as your fastest horse, followers had to be expected to think on their feet to carry out your mission.

Here is an accomplished military officer, with pre-Revolutionary War victories. He was literally the best chance the colonies had, and he says it is "absolutely necessary" that he have officers who could think for him.

That is a true sign of humility and leadership.

Washington's leadership style started with his character, which he had been working on since childhood. By the time the Revolutionary War broke out, Washington had spent many decades building his character and building his reputation among the other founding fathers.

Washington showed his future countrymen his character during the winter of 1777 to 1778 at Valley Forge. Farmers sold supplies to the British because the British paid in sterling silver. Privateers charged Washington a 1000 percent markup over what they charged civilians. He petitioned Congress for much-needed supplies. They authorized him to raid supplies from the public. He refused to do so because that was the type of tyranny he was fighting against.

Despite the hardships of Valley Forge, Washington instituted a training program that proved to be very successful, and in the spring Washington left Valley Forge with a much more disciplined army.

Here again, he relied on someone who knew more about military discipline than he did, Baron von Steuben, who literally wrote the book on American military discipline, *Regulations for the Order and Discipline of the Troops of the United States*. The book remained the drill manual for the United States military until 1812.

Who knows how the war might have played out but for the humility of Washington and his willingness to allow followers to think for him, and execute his orders.

Action Steps

As a leader, do you speak first in meetings? If you do, stop. Allow everyone else to speak first, from least senior to most. This encourages less senior people to speak their mind. Everyone gets a voice. As everyone speaks their mind, you can judge your ideas based on theirs. You may even hear a better idea that what you had in mind. By the end of the meeting, there should be a well-defined goal and several objectives.

Your people will like it because you took their input.

You look wise because you didn't have to say a word.

REFLECTIONS ON LEADERSHIP

The only true wisdom is in knowing you know nothing."

Socrates

When I started my current career, I thought I knew everything I needed to know about it. I had a BA, so what more did I need? Now seventeen years later, I have come to the conclusion that I don't know anything about my career field.

Don't get me wrong; I know a lot more now than I did then. I've read in the field and been to hundreds, if not thousands of hours of training. I have over three times more experience than the 10,000 hours rule. Yet I still feel that I don't know enough. So what do I do? I keep studying.

I am a lifelong student of everything. There is nothing I consider myself an expert in. Part of that is because I really don't feel that I am an expert. The other part is that there is danger in thinking you are expert in something.

Think about people you know who declare themselves expert in something. Are they really expert with no reason to continue studying the subject? Or is it just a story they tell themselves?

You've probably heard of the Dunning-Kruger effect. It's still worth providing a thumbnail sketch for people who don't know about it.

Social psychologists David Dunning and Justin Kruger describe a cognitive bias in which low performers believe they are expert at something. Their low self-awareness and low cognitive ability cause people to over-estimate their capabilities.

The effect also describes situations in which people are aware of their own expertise in an area. This awareness leads them to believe that their expertise extends to other areas.

Socrates recognized this same phenomenon, though it is not clear that he actually said the quote above. His student

REFLECTIONS ON LEADERSHIP

Plato may have invented the quote as a summation of Socrates' beliefs.

Socrates did say, "I do not think that I know what I do not know." I'm sure it rolls off the tongue better in Greek.

In *Apology,* Plato talks about Socrates' trial. During his testimony, Socrates says a friend of his asked the oracle at Delphi if anyone was wiser than Socrates. The oracle said no one was wiser than Socrates. Being a skeptical guy, Socrates asked the oracle the same question, and got the same answer.

Ever the skeptic, Socrates went on a quest to find the truth. He found people who were also wise, but those people assumed that their little bit of wisdom extended to areas that they knew nothing about.

In the face of this, Socrates admitted that the oracle was correct in that Socrates was wise enough to admit his own ignorance.

Socrates' trial took place in 399 B.C. Dunning and Kruger published their paper in 1999. It took just under 2400 years to prove that Socrates was correct.

That it took 2400 years to prove Socrates was correct is in itself a proof.

Social psychologists should have just asked philosophers because they call this "Socratic wisdom" or "Socratic ignorance."

Either way, Dunning-Kruger is nothing new, and neither is how you combat it.

When he heard what the oracle said, Socrates went to the oracle himself and did some research. You don't have to find an oracle for answers; just turn to the internet. If you are old-fashioned, find a book store. If you are really old, find a library. Whatever you do, always keep learning.

Next, he kept doing research. By talking to other wise people, Socrates sought to find someone wiser than himself.

We've already seen that not all wise people are wise in all areas. Remember, even if you are the smartest person in the room, everyone in the room knows something you don't.

Ask people how you are doing. Seek feedback. Even if you decide you don't want to use the advice, hearing another point of view forces you to evaluate your own.

Finally, Socrates evaluated what he learned and compared that to his own beliefs and thoughts. He questioned what he knew and asked himself if it was true.

REFLECTIONS ON LEADERSHIP

This was a man willing to believe, who wanted to believe there were people wiser than he was. And he was disappointed to find there were not.

We have all had leaders who suffer from Dunning-Kruger. You owe it to your followers to ensure that you do not.

As a rule, men worry more about what they can't see than about what they can."

Julius Caesar

Julius Caesar, the man so famous, that he is the man people think of when you say, "Caesar." In reality, Caesar was a title for Roman emperors, but it did not become a title for Roman emperors until after Julius Caesar. Emperors wanted to align themselves with him, so they took his name for their title. Until that time, Caesar was just a family name.

Judging from his life, Caesar did not worry about much. He was the first Roman general to cross the Rhine and the English Channel in the same year. He crossed both of these bodies of water to invade and send a message.

REFLECTIONS ON LEADERSHIP

Caesar crossed the Rhine to subdue Germanic tribes and show support for an ally. The tribes used the Rhine as a barrier, thinking it would stop invaders. Caesar wanted to cross it to send a message. His allied tribe offered to send boats. Caesar chose to build a bridge.

It sent the message that Rome could go anywhere it pleased. His army built the bridge in a few days. He took is men across it, burned some abandoned villages, then left and dismantled his bridge. The tribes had abandoned the villages because they were teaming up to fight him.

Caesar must have enjoyed his sojourn because he returned to the Rhine a few years later for a return engagement, with similar results. Again, he took his bridge with him when he left.

These antics and his military accomplishments earned Caesar a reputation that eventually caused fear in the Roman Senate.

Caesar had expanded Rome's boarders beyond Gaul. With the Gallic Wars over, the Senate told Caesar to disband his army and report to Rome. Caesar was part of the First Triumvirate, consisting of Pompey, Crassus, and Caesar. By this time, Crassus had died and Caesar suspected that Pompey had plans for him.

The Senate told him specifically not to cross the Rubicon with his army. The Senate should have known better than to tell Caesar not to cross a river: He seemed to have a thing for that.

In 49 B.C., Caesar took his army across the river and began his civil war. By 44 B.C., he was assassinated. It was a wild ride, during which he killed Pompey, was declared dictator a couple of times, met Cleopatra, defeated the pharaoh's army at the Battle of the Nile (what's with this guy and rivers?), and installed Cleopatra as ruler of Egypt. He returned to Rome, got bored, and went to the Middle East and destroyed the King of Pontus. Then he went to Africa and killed the last Senatorial supporters of Pompey.

Shortly after that, a group of Senators (including Brutus) got together and assassinated Caesar. His life had a brutal end, but none of it would have happened if he had been afraid of things he could not see.

Throughout his life, Caesar lived boldly. He expanded Rome's boarders. His Rhine crossing exploits so scared the Germans that they did not conduct any major incursions across the Rhine for several centuries. He would not have achieved if he had been afraid of things he could not see.

How do you live without fear like Caesar? Like with most of our problems, the first thing to do is to be aware of it. So

REFLECTIONS ON LEADERSHIP

many times people are not even aware of their own fear. They think they are acting out of some plan or instinct, when in reality they are afraid that something bad will happen. Become aware of the fear and create a plan to deal with it.

Caesar feared Pompey intended to harm him when he arrived in Rome, so he planned to take his army with him.

There are great big fears called phobias, and there are small fears, general anxieties that get in our way, preventing us from bring bold. A general strategy that helps with overall fear is to develop courage, which helps develop self-confidence, and can help in all areas of life.

Everyone possess courage in some measure. When you find that you have done something courageous, even if it is a small thing, recognize it. If you find that you have done one small thing in the face of a fear, say speaking to your crush without babbling incoherently, recognize that you took a step in building overall courage.

One of the best ways to develop courage and overcome fear is to do something every day that scares you. This has almost become cliché, yet there is a hint of truth to it. These do not have to be big things, like sky diving, or playing with tarantulas. These can be small things you do every day to help you develop courage.

DENNIS MOSSBURG

Say hi to strangers. Speak up in a meeting. Fail at something, anything, spectacularly, just fail at it so you know that you will survive failure. Ask your crush for a date. Interview for a job you have no hope of getting, just for the experience of interviewing.

Keep this up and you will soon be leading your crew around the forests of Germany, building bridges and tearing them down, just so you can say you can.

First say to yourself what you would be; and then do what you have to do."

Epictetus

Epictetus was a Greek Stoic philosopher, whose teaching influenced Marcus Aurelius.

He was born into slavery. If he was given a name at birth, it has been lost in time. He was born about 55 A.D., perhaps in Hierapolis, Phrygia. As the name suggests, Hierapolis was a Greek city, near modern Pamukkale, Turkey.

"Epiktetos" means "gained" or "acquired." According to Plato, the proper meaning of the name is "added to one's hereditary property."

He spent his youth in Rome as the slave of Epaphroditos, secretary to Nero. His owner allowed him to study philosophy, and his education gave him increased standing in society.

He gained his freedom sometime after Nero's death in 68 A.D. Having gained his freedom, Epictetus began teaching philosophy. Sometime around 93 AD, Emperor Domitian banished philosophers from the city, so Epictetus moved to Nicopolis in Greece.

As with many ancient philosophers, he has no known writings; all we know of his teachings is from one of his students, Arrian.

Epictetus seemed concerned with what we today call mindset. He argued that we have no power over things external to us, but our goals, the things inside us, should be what drive us. He viewed things in terms of choices and impressions.

When someone says something negative to us, or something positive to us, we cannot say it is bad or good, because they are external to us. These external things are impressions, and out of our control. If you place too much importance on impressions, you have given someone else control over you.

Epictetus says that you have control over how you respond to impressions. For him, the first step is to recognize that what someone has said is their opinion and out of your control. Next, ask if what is said is of value to you, then ask if the impression has to do with anything you can control or if it is beyond your control. If it is beyond your control, then let go of it.

In this way, we alone determine the good and bad of our actions. We should not try to impose our own ideas of good and bad on the actions of others, because their actions are beyond our control. In doing this, we may achieve peace of mind.

Epictetus' quote describes a two-step process. The first step is to identify what you want to be. That is a question everyone faces at some point, although some of us ask that question of ourselves several times in our lifetimes.

There is no single way to answer this question. There is no good way to answer this question, but I will offer a few suggestions.

Look at your hobbies. What are the things you like to do in your free time? What do you like to do to destress? What do you find joy in doing? These will give you an idea of what you want to do.

If this does not narrow down your focus or you want to get a second opinion, ask your friends about your friendship.

Ask them why you are friends. You will probably get some generic answers. Those are fine, because they get the conversation started and build a foundation. Start asking what you bring to the friendship that none of their other friends bring. Ask what role you play in their life.

Friends are better at sussing out those things we love to do than we are because they can be objective. They may even have told you in the past what you should do, but you did not believe them.

His second step is the solution to the first. You know what you want to do, but how do you do it?

His quote reminds me of advice given by various thought leaders that to achieve something, the best approach is to think about the type of person who achieves those things and be that person. If you want to be a CEO, ask yourself how a CEO acts, then do those things. If you want to be a world-famous writer, ask what you have to do to be that writer. Start by studying writers and do the things they do. What habits do famous writers have? Writing and dedication to the craft, not sitting around waiting for inspiration to strike. Successful writers do not spend time surfing the internet instead of writing. Writers write. To be a writer, get in the habit of writing; even if it is not very good, at least it gives you something to edit and maybe turn into something good.

REFLECTIONS ON LEADERSHIP

If you want to be an entrepreneur, ask yourself what entrepreneurs do. Many entrepreneurs tell you that their product or service came about because they were solving a problem for themselves, then realized that if they have the problem, it is likely that others have that same problem.

If you want to be an entrepreneur, think about the problems you have solved in your life, and find a way to solve the same problem in others' lives. There is more to it than that, of course, but this is where all entrepreneurs start: the idea.

Most people think that they cannot bring their idea to fruition because they do not have the money to do it. That is the wrong mindset. Epictetus tells you to do what you have to do. He does not say anything about getting out your checkbook.

I met a guy once who wanted to learn how to cook Italian food. He lived in a large city. He could have found a school that would have been glad to take his money and provide him with an education. What he did instead was go to a well-known local Italian restaurant and ask if he could volunteer to work there in exchange for an education in cooking Italian food. The restaurant was happy to do it because they always need workers.

My friend had to do some grunt work and things other than cooking, but his education was cheaper than paying for it.

We have a proof of concept; now what? Say you want to be an entrepreneur, so do what entrepreneurs do. That's great, but what do they do? I have found that entrepreneurs will tell you how they did it, and all you have to do is listen. But what do you do if you don't know any entrepreneurs? It's easy. Listen to podcasts, because lots of entrepreneurs are there. Read books; lots of entrepreneurs there. Go to the internet; lots of entrepre-neurs there too. Seek out local entrepreneurs and ask if you can volunteer at their organization. Seek opportunities to be around entrepreneurs, so you can learn what they do.

Remember my friend who wanted to be an Italian chef? You may have to do some grunt work, but you are getting an education. This will give you an opportunity learn what grunt work your organization will have to accomplish.

But this is a book about leadership, so what do you do if you want to be a leader? It's the same process, but you get more opportunities to practice. Again, you want to learn everything you can about leaders, through podcasts, books, magazines, and the internet. The good thing about leadership is that there are lots of leaders. We are surrounded by

REFLECTIONS ON LEADERSHIP

leaders. Every organization has leaders, both formal and informal.

Informal leaders are those people in an organization who have no formal authority, but because of technical skills, experience, or personality, their peers listen to their advice and follow their lead. This is where most leaders get their start, by being informal leaders.

If you want to gain leadership experience, begin by being an informal leader in your organization. Then follow up with a leader you trust and ask them if they would mentor you. Ask them for stretch assignments, ones that are just beyond your current abilities. By the time you complete the assignment, you will have the required skills and abilities.

When looking at leaders (or entrepreneurs), look at the negative examples as well as the positive ones. I have learned a lot about leadership from negative examples. If a negative leader makes you feel untrusted, unvalued, and unappreciated, remember that. Remember what they did. Remember how they made you feel, and vow that you will never make your followers feel the same way. Do that and you will be far ahead of many leaders.

Our friend Epictetus talked about mindset. Whatever you want to do is all about mindset. Tell yourself you can be an entrepreneur or a good leader and you can. Tell yourself this mantra as often as you can, and your mind will begin to look for what it takes to be that. When you start learning what it takes to be that, you will start being that.

REFLECTIONS ON LEADERSHIP

A sense of humor is part of the art of leadership, of getting along with people, of getting things done."

Dwight D. Eisenhower

Eisenhower was known for walking through the base camps talking with soldiers. He knew how to connect with them, he knew how to get along with people and how to get things done, and he knew the art of leadership. If Eisenhower felt a sense of humor is part of the art of leadership, who am I to argue?

People like people with a sense of humor, and they especially like people who do not take themselves too seriously. Develop a sense of humor and you will be one step closer to developing followers who will want to follow you.

If you are not a natural comedian, do not force it. Look for the humor in any situation. If you can, find ways to poke fun at yourself. This is disarming to people. If you do not take yourself too seriously, people will trust you. People who trust you will follow you.

Look for small gains. Do not try too hard. Read jokes, watch comedians, and look for chances to use their jokes, but again, do not overdo it. People are good at spotting fakes. If you try too hard, your followers will know and lose respect for you.

Still, you have to practice. If one joke does not land, the next one may, but do not try a steady stream of machine gun-fired jokes; that's trying too hard. If a joke does not land, move on. Do not make a big deal about it.

Stay positive and laugh. People want to be around people who laugh. If people are already in a good mood, they are more likely to find humor in situation or find jokes as funny. Being positive and laughing prime the pump for humor.

Witty beats silly. Wit requires spontaneity, so again, you have to look for humor in all situations. If you know some witty people, spend time with them exchanging jabs, but

REFLECTIONS ON LEADERSHIP

remember that the point is to have fun. Do not get mean. If you feel your sparring partner lands a hit below the belt, do not take it personally; just roll with it. Developing a sense of humor is easier when you can forgive people, especially if you both were intending to have fun. If you feel you are in over your head, use your emotional intelligence and throw in the towel, but make a plan to come back better armed.

Tell funny stories about your day. If you have been looking for funny things in your life, this should become easy. I told my staff a story about a lesson learned,

One day, I walked up to one of my staff and issued directions for the day. I had not seen that staff member yet that day. As I'm giving the instructions, I notice a look of consternation on his face. What he's upset about is not immediately apparent, at least not to me.

I kept talking, but the look was not leaving his face. Something was very wrong, but I could not put my finger on it.

Had I forgotten deodorant? Don't check.

Was there dog hair on my shirt? I have a German Shepard, and her hair sticks to everything. Don't brush it off. Body language experts say that means I am brushing off the person I am talking to.

Did I have something in my teeth? I resisted the urge to check.

Then it hit me.

I stopped mid-sentence, and gave a little sigh.

"How's your day?" I asked. He smiled then started talking. We talked a few minutes. When the conversation lulled, I asked, "Can I tell you what I was going to have you do?" The staff member laughed and said I could.

I don't remember what I had to tell him that was so important, and I do not remember what he had done that day, but I remember how he looked at me. And I remember the difference a simple question made. Now, I always make it a point to make a personal connection with my staff before I make a professional one.

REFLECTIONS ON LEADERSHIP

Earn your leadership every day."

Michael Jordan

Jordan is well known for his skills and abilities on the basketball court. I am not even a basketball fan and cannot say with any confidence that I watched him play, but his record speaks for itself.

He won six NBA championships, six Finals Most Valuable Player Awards, and many other basketball accolades.

There is no doubt that Jordan possessed the technical skills for his chosen profession, but leaders require more than that. His coach, Phil Jackson, taught Jordan the value of strengthening his bonds with his teammates. Jackson knew that as good as Jordan was, he could not carry a team alone; he needed exceptional teammates.

As Jordan matured as a player, he learned the value of his teammates, trusting them with opportunities to make the game-winning shots.

Jordan put in the effort to get to know his teammates on and off the court. The bonds he developed off the court resulted in better bonds on the court. Jordan's exceptional abilities elevated the play of his teammates. They believed in him, so they played better themselves. His trust in them made them trust themselves.

Jordan learned that leadership was not a one-and-done event. You can be the most trusted, most respected, most admired leader, but if you do not show your followers every day that you trust, respect, and admire them, you will not be their leader for long.

Leadership comes in small signs that you are making the effort every day to prove your trust, respect, and admiration. Below are some suggestions for you to incorporate into everyday leadership.

Be adaptable. Every day brings new challenges. If you act as if each new challenge is the end of the world, your followers will not believe you know what you are doing. Worse, they will act like every new challenge is the end of the world, and your organization will be in a constant state of crisis. No organization can grow in that environment.

REFLECTIONS ON LEADERSHIP

Remember, no battle plan survives first contact with the enemy. Know that this is true outside of the military. You have to be willing to adapt your plans to whatever the reality is. Plan for things not to go right and learn to roll with the punches.

Be careful about being too reactionary. Your followers and organization will not tolerate a leader who changes course with each change in wind direction.

One way to keep from being too reactionary is to have a clear vision. Your followers should know from your every action and word what your vision is. They should never feel that your vision and values have changed. Having a clear vision keeps you moving in the correct direction, even as you adapt to new realities.

Leaders show up. Know your followers. Be there for them. Show up for the big events. If our organization has multiple shifts, show up for the shift you do not usually work.

I interned at a sheriff department. One day the sheriff told me that when he was first elected, he went to a rollcall to meet his deputies. When he walked in the room, everyone fell silent. He knew immediately that however the previous sheriff led his department, it had not resulted in a healthy work environment. He knew at that moment that he had to show up more and be more available for his deputies to help change that environment.

Emotional intelligence is a way of understanding your own feelings and those of others, not so that you can succumb to them or manipulate others, but so you can better understand yourself and others. If you can learn to recognize your own feelings and identify the triggers for these feelings, you can help prevent yourself from over-reacting to the ever-changing realities of life.

Emotional intelligence is also the ability to empathize with others. Followers trust leaders with who show empathy. Leaders who recognize the emotions of their followers are trusted by the followers. I am not suggesting that you become a nursemaid or therapist. I am suggesting that you acknowledge that your followers are human and that sometimes they need allowances for the realities of their lives.

Emotional intelligence does not suggest that you suppress your emotions, but to leverage them for your betterment, and more important, the betterment of your team.

I cannot promise that earning your leadership every day will make you a six-time NBA champion, but it will make your team feel like all of you are.

REFLECTIONS ON LEADERSHIP

There is a difference between being a leader and being a boss. Both are based on authority. A boss demands blind obedience; a leader earns his authority through understanding and trust."

Klaus Balkenhol

Balkenhol is an Olympic equestrian. He won a gold medal in 1992 Olympics in Barcelona, Spain, for the German team. He has also trained the U.S. Olympic team and is the writer of several equestrian books.

Too many people think that they earn their leadership through promotion and rank. That is simply not true. Anyone can attain a rank. People like to argue about how many types of authority there are. For the sake of this, I'm going to talk about three: positional, expert, and relationship.

I once worked in a paramilitary organization. I was having a discussion about leadership with someone one rank above me. Finally, in exasperation, I pointed to the rank insignia on my collar and said, "This is not a decoration." The person I was talking to became very upset.

This is an example of positional authority. This type of person maintains their control through their position. To them, building relationships is not as important as ensuring people follow orders. This is one of the least-effective methods of leadership. There are times it is necessary, but there are often better tools in the toolbox.

Expert authority is just what it sounds like. This person is a technical expert in their field, so followers follow because they have confidence in the leader. This is a good tool and should be used to gain confidence in your followers. Its effectiveness may be limited in less-technical environments, though.

Finally, relationship authority is when the leader may or may not be an expert, but they are at least competent. They have worked on relationships. They know their weaknesses and strengths and those of their followers.

They use relationships to achieve the mission. Their followers follow because they trust the leader. The leader is

REFLECTIONS ON LEADERSHIP

not the expert in the field, but the leader knows how to get the best out of people and how to communicate the vision.

There is a time and a place for each of these types of authority. Most experts, and Balkenhol, agree that the one a leader needs to rely on the most is relationship.

To Balkenhol, a boss is the positional leader, while the leader is relational. Balkenhol talks about understanding and trust. You have to have trust to get on a thousand-pound animal that can gallop at 30 miles an hour.

Horses understand rank and position; that's how their herds are organized. A human being will never be able to out-muscle a horse. It is possible for a human to bully a horse, but in this situation, horses (and humans) will only work hard enough to keep the bully away from them. That's at best; at worst, a horse might fight back.

An equestrian works on building trust and understanding with their teammate. So should leaders.

Action Steps

- Be firm, fair, and consistent.
- Monitor progress and reward with encouraging messages. Support words with actions.

- Refrain from shaming and controlling discipline practices.
- Focus the message on behaviors.
- Care about your people and avoid dominating them.
- Ask if what you are doing is for you or your followers.
- Recognize when your use of power is doing harm to your followers.

REFLECTIONS ON LEADERSHIP

A leader isn't someone who forces others to make him stronger; a leader is someone willing to give his strength to others so that they may have the strength to stand on their own."

Beth Revis

Revis is the author of young adult science fiction and fantasy novels.

Being a leader is about strength, but not in the sense that you have to be strong enough to force compliance; that is a mistake. As a leader, you have to be strong enough to bear the burden of leading. As a leader, you have to accept that you are responsible for making others better. You are responsible for another person's well-being and safety, one shift at a time.

People sell portions of their life to an organization in exchange for a promise. That promise is different in each organization, but the root is some sort of security or peace. Time is precious. As technologically advanced as we are becoming, one thing we cannot create is more time. An organization should not take for granted that people will always be willing to sell their time to the organization. Organizations should be humbled that people would be willing to participate in the transaction.

As a leader, you should feel the burden to build the strength of each of your followers. To do this, you will have to give some of your strength to make your followers better. It can be a long process, but you want your followers to be strong enough that they can stand on their own. Without that ability, leaders will be propping up their followers.

The equation is simple: Spend your strength in strengthening your followers or spend your strength in propping them up. In the first scenario, you give up your strength for a short time. In the second, you give up your strength for as long as the follower stays at your organization.

Now who is giving up their precious time for the organization?

REFLECTIONS ON LEADERSHIP

Action Steps

Begin every day with one of these questions. When you answer them honestly and act on them, then you will begin to give your strengths to others.

- What are your strengths?
- How can you help others?
- Who you can help?
- What is your pro-social motivation?

Remember, teamwork begins by building trust. And the only way to do that is to overcome our need for invulnerability."

Patrick Lencioni

Lencioni is the author of 11 books on business, management, and leadership. He is also the president of a management consulting firm.

There is that word again: trust. Lencioni's plan for developing trust is to overcome our need to be invulnerable. There are many definitions of invulnerable, including "incapable of being wounded, hurt or damaged" and "proof against or immune to attack."

I hate to break it to you, but we are all vulnerable. We can all be wounded, hurt, or damaged. None of us are

REFLECTIONS ON LEADERSHIP

immune to attacks, especially in business. Business is a realm in which some cultures – not all – seem bent on destroying themselves in the name of metrics, dashboards, and key performance indicators.

Those are just numbers. They have no feeling for people. These measurements do not care about you, and yet some people are obsessed with them. It is a one-way relationship. Some business leaders and managers are in love with these numbers, numbers that can never love them. They love these numbers at the expense of their relationships with people who actually have the capacity to love them back.

We are all vulnerable to this type of manager. We can all be wounded, harmed, or damaged by people who are in love with metrics. So pretending we are invulnerable is a fool's errand. How do we protect ourselves from becoming this type of manager? By building trust. How do we build trust? By admitting that we are vulnerable. By admitting that we need help. By admitting that we can help each other. This sounds as though the follower needs to build the trust ... not the manager.

Needing help is not the same thing as being helpless. Helpless can be defined as an inability to act or react, or deprived of strength or power. We know that leaders, the right kind of leaders, have power, the right kind of power.

The kind of power that is derived from the goodwill and trust of those who follow them. The kind of power that causes others to follow you because they trust you will protect them.

Action Steps

- Give credit where credit is due.
- Admit mistakes.
- Tackle the difficult issues.
- Have the difficult conversations.
- Listen to others when they talk about their problems, even if those problems are not about work. This builds trust. If you are more about logic, then consider this: If your employee's problems are affecting their performance, then your listening helps their performance.
- Discuss behaviors, not motivations. We often misunderstand our own motives, so why do we think we can understand someone else's? People can argue with you about their motives, but they cannot argue about their behaviors.

REFLECTIONS ON LEADERSHIP

Successful leaders see the opportunities in every difficulty rather than the difficulty in every opportunity"

Reed Markham

Leaders have to be optimistic. As every veteran has heard, no battle plan survives first contact with the enemy. Whether in combat or not, plans rarely work out exactly the way they are written out. Leaders have to know the value in seeing opportunities and how to take advantage of them.

Pessimists are not going to see what can be salvaged when things go wrong; they are going to succumb to their negativity bias and only look at what has been lost rather than what is to be gained.

Leaders not only have to worry about what can be gained or salvaged from bad situations, they need to realize that their followers watch everything they do. If followers suspect that their leader will fold like a lawn chair at the first hint of trouble, they will not trust the leader in hard times. If they do not trust their leader in hard times, the leader will hardly be trusted in good times.

Leadership aside, our overall health is impacted by our optimism or pessimism. Psychologists define pessimism as the tendency to think about adverse events in a way that makes them feel powerless. This mindset places us in a position that makes it harder to overcome the adversity. That a pessimist believes that they are powerless in the face of adversity sets them up to think that whatever they do to surmount the adversity will fail.

Pessimists are more at risk for developing post-traumatic stress and depression when they face adversity and for losing motivation when they fail.

The good news is that pessimism and optimism can be can be learned. So how do you learn to be an optimist? There are many options; here are a few that I have had success with.

Show gratitude. This can take several forms. One way is to simply thank people for the things they have done for you.

REFLECTIONS ON LEADERSHIP

Another is to keep a gratitude journal. This does not have to be a long journaling exercise. It only takes a few minutes. I write about at least one thing I am grateful for every day. Some days, admittedly, I am grateful simply for being alive, and some days that is enough. Other days, I easily write a couple of hundred words for the happening in my life. That is the way of things. Progress, however small, is still progress.

Watch your self-talk. Negative self-talk sets us up for failure. The words we tell ourselves are the words our minds focus on. Tell yourself that you are a failure, and your mind starts thinking that you are and starts working at ways to torpedo your efforts. It also sets you up for selective attention where you only notice and fixate on the times you fail and do not give enough attention to the times you succeed.

This is the same principle that causes you to see the same model of car again and again when you are interested in buying one. It's not that hundreds of others have just decided to buy the same car. You have told your mind that you are interested in that car, so it wants to tell you that the cars are you are looking for are available. Your mind is looking for those cars because you told it you wanted it to. The same is true for gratitude.

If we are truly the average of the five people we spend the most time with, then be careful about who you spend time with, especially if they are pessimists. Try to spend time with optimists or recognize when your pessimist friends are leading you down a negative path and find a detour.

There was a guy I used to work with regularly who could be the most negative guy I ever talked to. I worked with him a few times before I recognized the effect he was having on me. At the end of our shift, I often felt run down and worn out. There were a few occasions when I did not feel that way after working with him. I looked back at how we spent out shift together, and I realized that the shifts where I felt miserable were the shifts he was especially negative.

I quickly developed a strategy where I started the shift on a positive note. I made sure to talk about the topics I knew he enjoyed and was careful not to talk about things I knew were hot button topics for him. The end result is that I never had another negative shift with him. Not that every shift went smoothly, but the bad events seemed to hold less power over me.

Setting goals and priorities is one of the most important things you can do to create optimism. Setting goals, real important goals, goals that you live and dream for will give you the motivation to keep moving forward. When you have

REFLECTIONS ON LEADERSHIP

a clear idea of what you want and you review your goals regularly, it seems like everything you do helps push you to that goal. This is the corollary to the negative self-talk above, only this is part of positive self-talk.

You have told yourself that you are going to achieve your goals, so when you encounter adversity, you mind knows it is supposed to help you reach your goal. It then looks for other ways to achieve them; it looks for a detour around the adversity.

For the sake of your team and your health, learn to see the opportunities in every difficulty.

Lead by inspiration, not intimidation."

Rebecca Aguilar

Aguilar's CV includes freelance reporter, social media columnist, and motivational speaker among other vocations. She has been working as a journalist since 1981.

Her quote succinctly summarizes one of the basic tenets of leadership: Inspire your followers. If you have properly inspired them, there is no need for intimidation because they are already working toward the vision you have painted for them.

How well does intimidation work anyway? We have all experienced intimidation in one way or another, and whether we want to admit it, we have all succumbed to

REFLECTIONS ON LEADERSHIP

intimi-dation at some point. Sometimes it has happened in childhood, in school, at work, we may have even experienced it on the roadway. How did you feel afterward? Probably not great. You probably felt like doing the exact opposite of what the intimidator wanted you to do. Even if you succumbed to the intimidation, did you feel like going out of your way to help the person later? Did you feel like spending any time with them?

Leaders who use intimidation create followers who do not feel safe at work. Their followers do not feel valued, and they do not feel motivated to work hard for the organization.

There is much in the news in the last few years about intimidation of children in school: bullying. We decry it in schools, but accept it in organizations. Somehow it is not OK to bully our children, but it is acceptable to bully our followers. What kind of messages are we sending to our children? We tell them not to be bullies at school, and we give them solutions and support, then we come home and complain about our toxic boss. What message are our children receiving? The one we want them to hear or the one we are living?

What if you are a toxic boss who rules through intimidation, but tells your children not to be bullied. How do you reconcile those two behaviors? Do you even recognize your behaviors are toxic?

Here are some signs that a boss is toxic. If you find that any of these apply to you, you may want to reevaluate your leadership practices.

Your boss is critical all the time: A leader needs to evaluate staff performance and looks for ways to get the most out of their followers, but the negativity bias ensures that people tend to focus on the negative and are much harder on themselves than you can be. Find the things your staff are doing well and focus on that behavior. There are times that poor performance needs to be addressed, and real leaders address the behavior and move on. Remember on page 11 where I talked about the ideal positive to negative feedback ratios ranging from 3:1 to 6:1? Good leaders do not hold poor performance over their followers like the sword of Damocles, just waiting to drop it on them at every opportunity.

Your boss has unpredictable mood swings: People like stability. Leaders who are predictable in their actions are easier to work with. Learning emotional intelligence helps you learn how to keep your mood swings in check.

Your boss micromanages: If you are a micromanager, stop it now, for the sake of your staff and your own mental health. If you are a micromanager, you are adding unnecessary stress to yourself and your followers. Micromanagers make their followers stop thinking. If they know you are going to tell them every step to take, then why should they bother thinking? Asking for progress reports is not micromanaging. Telling followers how to perform every little task is.

Your boss disappears: This is the opposite of a micromanager. In leadership theory, this is called laissez-faire leadership. This leader does not answer emails. Does not offer advice. Does not provide any training. Does not help their followers in any way. Effective leaders learn to strike a balance between micromanaging and laissez-faire managing. Leaders have to be in the Goldilocks zone of leadership: not too much and not too little management.

Your boss refuses to listen to you: We have seen in other entries that leaders need to listen to their followers. Followers are often closer to the work and more aware of potential problems. This also makes them better able to provide an effective solution to the problem. Followers who help create the plan are more invested in the plan.

Your boss pits follower against follower: This is the old divide-and-conquer theme of leadership. As a leader, you have a team to lead. Pitting your team against each other undermines them and eventually you.

Your boss gaslights you and others. The phrase comes from the play and two movies all of the same name, *Gaslight*. It is a form of manipulation wherein the manipulator tries to convince their victim that they cannot trust their own memory, judgment, and perceptions. The goal is to lower self esteem and create dependency on the manipulator.

All of these are signs that a boss uses intimidation to lead. So what can you do to be more inspiring? Here are a few suggestions.

Have a clear set of mission, vision, and values. This helps followers know what their objectives are, where the ship is headed. It also helps if you have mood swings. If you remember what your vision, mission, and values are and you live up to those, your mood should stabilize because you are focused on what is important.

Create stretch goals for your followers: These allow your followers to hit achievable goals. These goals are just out of reach of a follower's current abilities and help them develop and grow those skills and abilities.

REFLECTIONS ON LEADERSHIP

Encourage self-development: Encourage your followers to have goals and help them achieve them. Followers want to know that they are valued. Helping them achieve their goals is one of the best ways to show them that they matter to you and the organization. Additionally, if they know you are helping them, they will be more likely to help you.

Listen to your followers. This tactic has appeared in other areas of this book. It must be important. I am reminded of the adage that you have two ears and one mouth, which means that you have to listen twice as much as you talk. Listen to your followers; if they trust you, they will help steer you clear of troubles.

Inspiration literally means "divine guidance." Intimidate means "to frighten or make afraid."

Would you rather be a bully or divine?

Courage is what it takes to stand up and speak; courage is also what it takes to sit down and listen."

Winston Churchill

Churchill was a great orator; he knew how to use the language. He knew how to create a vision of what could be, and he gave listeners and followers the inspiration they needed to help achieve his vision.

Churchill was an expert at employing Saint-Exupéry's quote about teaching followers to yearn for the sea to inspire followers to build a boat.

His speeches during World War II are inspiring. In the "We shall fight on the beaches" speech, he famously used imagery to boost the morale of his countrymen and

REFLECTIONS ON LEADERSHIP

his military to strike fear in his enemies, and to try to goad the international community into action.

Some of his less-serious quotes carry a serious message, with his tongue firmly planted in his cheek.

This one talks about courage and what it takes to have courage. The funny thing is that courage can sometimes require opposite actions.

The first part of the quote is talking about standing up and speaking for what you believe in. His wartime speeches are a perfect example of this, a time when some politicians felt that appeasing Hitler was the only road to peace. Churchill knew that Hitler was not likely to stop. Churchill needed the courage to stand up in the face of
those in the appeasement crowd and convince his fellow politicians, and the king, that appeasement was the road to destruction for their island.

He also had the courage to stand up to Hitler and tell him (through the speeches) that the United Kingdom was not going to be an easy target like some of the European nations were.

But there were a few other stakeholders Churchill wished to reach: potential allies. He was hoping to gain support from the United States and other sympathetic countries to come to the United Kingdom's aid. He wanted potential allies to know that the United Kingdom was not going to just roll over, and it was not going to be the damsel in distress, standing by watching her hero save the day. Churchill wanted the world to know that the United Kingdom was not going to back down, and if others came to its aid, maybe together, they could end the threat posed by Hitler.

The second part of the quote is the less obvious, less serious, but no less an important part. Leadership does not always require grand oration; sometimes it requires silence. We have examined this elsewhere in this book, but it is important enough to explore again.

Leaders need to listen to their followers. Not just listen to, but hear what they are saying and what they are not saying, and sometimes that takes courage. After all, we are leaders. We do not have to listen to anyone. We know it all already, right? It's going to be impossible to know it all.

Leaders must have the courage to listen to their followers; they often have good ideas because they are not us. They are probably detached; they do not have an emotional investment clouding their vision. They look at the situation with fresh eyes. They will think about the problem differently.

REFLECTIONS ON LEADERSHIP

Listening can be scary. We are leaders; we know it all. In listening, we may discover that our assumptions were wrong. The problem may not be what we thought it was. Our problem may not be as easy to solve as we thought it would be. We may find out that we do not know as much about the problem as we thought we did.

We may just find out that we were wrong. Willingness to discover that takes courage.

Also, followers are closer to the problem than we are. This is the classic problem with a top-down hierarchy: All the authority is at the top of the organizational chart, but the knowledge is at the bottom of the chart. Followers are nearest to the problem, so they have a much clearer idea of the solution than we do.

Finally, listening to and hearing your followers tells them that you trust them. If you really hear them, you have established a level of trust because you are showing them that you value their opinion; you genuinely want to hear what they have to say and think. This goes beyond the nodding "How are you?" conversation many followers have with their leaders. This is a conversation of substance that will actually have an impact on the job and on their lives.

Listening to them shows that you want to help them have a better work life, which leads to a better life.

As a follower, it is much easier to accept the work you have to do if you are part of the solution. It is no longer the boss's problem; it is your problem. If you are solving the boss's problem, then you do not care if you get a solution. All you care about is doing your eight and hitting the gate.

If you are solving your problem, well now, that is different. A follower who sees the problem as his problem wants to solve it.

Have the courage to sit down, shut up, and listen to your followers. You will be surprised at how much they know and care.

Action Steps

Watch body language. Closing-off behaviors like crossing arms or legs indicate discomfort. It may be because of something you said, or that they had too many tacos.

Covering your mouth is a sign that you are trying to hold words in. I once stopped in a coworker's office to say good morning. I had a friendly, bantering relationship with this person. When I entered the office, I started in with a "Good morning," but stopped when his hand flew to his mouth. I told him about what that meant and asked what he was holding in.

REFLECTIONS ON LEADERSHIP

He laughed and said, "I was going to say, 'It's too early.' "

Listen for paraverbals, tone inflections, changes in cadence, and pitch. As an exercise, say, "I didn't say you were wrong" multiple times, each time placing the emphasis on a different word. Each time you say it, you find the sentence has a different meaning.

Ask questions. Do not ask why, because it creates defensiveness. Asking why implies that you are placing blame. *How* and *what* questions are much better.

Summarize what they have said. Summarizing helps establish that you understood what they told you. I have found the following prompt useful: "What I hear you saying is ... "

The good will of the governed will be starved if not fed by the good deeds of the governors."

Ben Franklin

F ew will debate that Franklin was a wise man. Many of his quotes are still remembered today. Though he was never a President of the country, it is fair to say that he was instrumental to the creation and stabilization of the United States. Without his work as an ambassador and statesman, it is difficult to calculate where this country would be now.

One can look at this quote literally or figuratively. When in Ireland, Franklin noticed the effects of English policies and laws on the Irish people. The level of poverty he saw

REFLECTIONS ON LEADERSHIP

reminded him of what Americans faced if they did not do something about colonial exploitation by the British.

His literal point is clear: If the government does not take care of and feed its people, its people will not have goodwill for the government and will look for ways to throw off the government shackles.

Franklin drew parallels between what he saw in Ireland and the North American colonies. He used literal words to describe a philosophical event. The Irish people were starving to death and losing their goodwill toward the crown.

This quote does not have to be taken literally. Organizations sometimes think that the only way to reward followers is with money, medical coverage, and retirement. Those inducements go a long way, but how many unhappy followers would be happier if their organization did nothing more than treat their followers with respect?

I have taken pay cuts to work for organizations that promised more respect and growth opportunities. Sometimes a cut in pay is worth the stress reduction.

Does it really cost anything to treat your followers better? I'm not talking about Google-like campuses with kitchens, playrooms, nap areas, and gymnasiums. I'm just talking about treating your followers like you trust them.

The cost of treating your followers well has to be calculated differently than with a simple balance sheet. It is easy to calculate the cost of hiring and training employees. If you do offer some basic amenities, like a workout area, you can throw that cost in too.

How do you calculate the cost of lost innovation? How do you calculate the loss to your organization when employees no longer feel valued and work just hard enough to keep their jobs? How do you calculate the costs of genuinely gifted employees who leave your organization and take their good ideas with them?

Where does that complex calculus fit in to your simple balance sheet? Does this type of math even compute with some organizations? It does not have to be complex. Properly executed flexible work schedules, the ability to work from home, employee-recognitions programs, increased training opportunities, and education-reimbursement programs have all shown to be popular employee benefits.

Pay and benefits go a long way to feeding followers, but Maslow showed us that people are fed by much more than mere material goods.

REFLECTIONS ON LEADERSHIP

If you fail to recognize that, you may end up like the crown and the colonies: a superior power left with egg on their face, wondering what the hell happened.

I can't expect loyalty from the army if I do not give it."

George C. Marshall

There is a view of how military leaders lead. When people think of military leadership, they often think of R. Lee Ermey's tough, no-nonsense persona that he made famous in *Full Metal Jacket.* Do not misunderstand: I enjoyed watching his performance in the movie, and I enjoyed watching him carry on that persona on many other television shows.

However, the more I read about military leaders who have led troops into combat, who have given orders that have resulted in deaths, the more I have learned that military leadership is more than that.

REFLECTIONS ON LEADERSHIP

I am sure that Ermey's drill instructor persona is accurate. I have spoken to enough veterans to know that Ermey's portrayal was true to life of drill instructors (little surprise since Ermey was one). Reading about military leadership outside boot camp makes me think that the leadership style begins to change when leaders have to put leadership into action.

General Marshall is no exception. Marshall was the Chief of Staff under Franklin D. Roosevelt and Harry Truman. He later became the Secretary of State, then Secretary of Defense for Truman. It was his plan, the Marshall Plan, that provided the framework and money for the reconstruction of Europe after World War II. For his efforts, Marshall earned the Nobel Peace Prize in 1956.

Marshall's military résumé begins in 1902 when he was commissioned as a Second Lieutenant, and "ends" in 1945. I used quotation marks because Marshall resigned from the Joint Chiefs of Staff, but he did not retire. He was a Five Star General, a General of the Army. As such, he would remain on active duty for the rest of his life.

His military résumé is impressive. He served in the Philippine–American War and during both World Wars. In addition to commanding soldiers, he was also responsible for 35 Civilian Conservation Corp camps in southern Washington and Oregon.

The CCC was a make-work program during the depression. Marshall saw the program as a way to build relationships with the civilian population and to give the CCC volunteers valuable job skills.

On a side note, I have lived most of my life in Washington and Oregon, where much of the infrastructure work of the CCC still stands today. It was an impressive program, and Marshall's work had a lasting impact on the area. Much of the infrastructure we see includes rock walls built by hand in state and national parks. That is not all the CCC did, but it is one of the most recognizable examples that the CCC left behind. The work was labor-intensive and often done in poorly accessible areas.

Ordering around troops is one thing; they have to do what you say. Creating a vision for civilian volunteers compelling enough to build infrastructure that is still standing 83 years later is impressive.

Marshall and his wife visited the CCC camps. He said the whole assignment was, "the most instructive service I ever had, and the most interesting."

REFLECTIONS ON LEADERSHIP

Marshall talks about loyalty and having to give it before you can get it. We see that he also applied that theory to the CCC.

In World War I, Marshall was involved in the Battle of Cantigny. While planning for the battle, Marshall was riding his horse from the division headquarters to several subordinate units to check in with the soldiers there and conduct pre-attack coordination.

Marshall's horse stumbled, fell, and rolled over on Marshall, severely spraining and bruising his right foot. Marshall had a doctor bind and treat his leg there, so he did not have to report for a physical examination that would have removed him from battle.

Marshall's loyalty was to the soldiers. He could have easily thought only of himself and avoided the upcoming battle, but he wanted to be with the troops and oversee the execution of the plan he helped develop. He understood that to gain loyalty from his troops, he had to give it to them first.

Action Steps

Live your organization's mission, vision, and values.

Allow employees doing the work to plan the tactics for your goals and objectives.

Mentor and coach employees. This means teaching them the skills they need to be promoted. Do not make what it takes to be promoted a secret. Do not trust your employees to just tumble upon the qualities you are looking for.

REFLECTIONS ON LEADERSHIP

The troops, the air, and the Navy did all that bravery and devotion to duty could do. If any blame or fault attaches to the attempt, it is mine alone."

General Eisenhower

This line was from Eisenhower's "in case of failure" contingency D-Day message. I have spoken at length about Eisenhower's leadership; therefore, I will be brief on this one, but this quote that never was is worth looking at.

Eisenhower wrote a letter the day before the invasion where he took responsibility for the failure of the landing. As we all know, the landing was not a failure; still, he was ready to take the blame. Not only was he willing to take the blame, he was unequivocally taking the blame. Because he wrote this the day before the invasion, there was no way to know which part or parts of the plan might fail, but that did not matter to Eisenhower, because as the leader, everything was his fault.

He recognized that, using the phrase "it is mine alone" when talking about blame.

I cannot find a single reference to Eisenhower taking credit for D-Day. It may exist, but I doubt it. Eisenhower's "failure letter" is readily available on the internet, but there is no reference to Eisenhower taking credit.

That's because Eisenhower, the leader that he was, knew that he gets the blame for failure and the troops get the credit for success.

Action Steps

Eisenhower displayed humility. Here are tips to become more humble.

- Admit when you are wrong.
- Be grateful for and to your followers.
- Recognize your faults (believe me, you have them).

REFLECTIONS ON LEADERSHIP

- Recognize that not everyone thinks and does things the same way you do.

- Accept that you are your only competition.

Say not always what you know, but always know what you say."

Claudius

Claudius was an interesting figure, and this is an interesting quote. It talks about deception and not deception. When you know more about Claudius, the quote makes more sense.

His journey to becoming the Roman emperor was not an easy one. He lived from August 1, 10 B.C. to October 13, 54 A.D., in Gaul. His father was stationed there as a military legate. Claudius was the first emperor born outside of Rome.

As with many Roman emperors, his history is full of intrigue. He was a sickly child with a limp and slight deafness. This led to many difficulties in his life, but may

REFLECTIONS ON LEADERSHIP

have ultimately led to his becoming emperor. When his family learned of his infirmities, they more or less cast him aside, paying little attention to him.

During the reigns of Tiberius and Caligula, purges resulted in the deaths of many nobles. These purges always seemed to pass him over, perhaps because no one saw him as a threat. In fact, during the Caligula purge, the Praetorian Guard named him emperor mostly because there were no more male heirs to the throne. It is a little more compli-cated than that, but this is the short story.

Reading his history, you have to wonder at what point in his life did Claudius learn about deception, for it is said that once he was emperor, his many frailties either disappeared or diminished.

Being a Roman emperor, he was the target of several attempts on his life and attempted coups; despite this, he was one of the longest reigning Roman emperors at 13 years. When he finally did die, it was probably due to poisoning, probably at the
hands of his fourth wife.

The first part of Claudius' quote suggests deception: "say not always what you know." This could mean don't volunteer information; it could also mean don't always tell every-thing you know, though that suggests the lie of omission.

There are times when it is best not to volunteer information, even in leadership. Little white lies are the lubrication of social discourse. Do you always want to tell your spouse the truth, the whole truth, and nothing but the truth? This seems like a good idea, until you employ it.

If you doubt me, try telling your wife that she is wrong about anything. Rule number one to a successful marriage is that your wife is never wrong, even when she is.

In marriage and leadership, truth is of the utmost importance, but so is maintaining lines of communication. If it means not fully disclosing information, then so be it.

The second part of the quote is equally important: "but always know what you say." This part suggests that while the lie of omission may be OK in some circumstances, the lie of commission is not. Do not tell people things that you know are false.

Human interactions are messy. We are controlled by emotions and body chemicals most of us are not aware of. Dopamine, serotonin, oxytocin, and endorphins all control our emotions and lives in ways that we often don't

REFLECTIONS ON LEADERSHIP

recognize. Sometimes we react in ways that even we cannot predict.

We often can forgive and even understand lies of omission. If we were in a similar situation and wanted to spare another person's feelings, we can understand that; we may even do that same thing ourselves.

Lies of commission we find much harder to forgive. Tell your followers what you know. If you do not know the answer to their question, tell them, but also tell them that you will find out and that when you find out, you will let them know.

Be true to your word. Do not make promises you cannot keep.

This is also an admonition not to gossip. If you do not know something to be true, then don't talk about it. If you need to talk about it, find out the truth. Tell your followers only those things that you know.

If you suspect something to be true, and you feel your followers must know, then preface what you are saying.

Oftentimes followers want to know where an organization is headed. With a lack of complete information, you may want to tell them what you think will happen, but ensure you tell them that what you are saying is your suspicion based on fact, past practice, and other information.

They trust you as their leader because of your past knowledge and wisdom. Uncertainty, makes people nervous, but telling them what may happen can put them at ease, especially if your past theories can come true.

Allaying your followers' fears is an important role. So is giving wise counsel. If you find that you are no good at predicting the future, do not offer predictions; just say you do not know and leave it at that.

To tell your followers something, only for them to find out it is not true is a sure way to lose their trust and respect.

Always know what you tell them.

REFLECTIONS ON LEADERSHIP

If you find yourself in a fair fight, you didn't plan your mission properly."

David Hackworth

Hackworth was a military journalist and a veteran who served in World War II, the Korean War, and the Vietnam War. At 14, Hackworth lied about his age and paid a transient to pose as his father to say the Hackworth was old enough to join the Merchant Marines. One year later in 1946, he returned home, then used his Merchant Marine paperwork to convince the U.S. Army that he was old enough to join.

He was assigned to post-World War II Italy where he earned his General Education Diploma. He was a sergeant during the Korean War, and in 1951 he received a battlefield promotion to second lieutenant. Then after a successful raid, he received a promotion to first lieutenant.

The Army offered him the opportunity to lead a new unit, and he created the 27th Wolfhound Raiders. At the end of his tour, he volunteered for another tour and was promoted to captain.

He was demobilized due to the armistice, but after two years as a civilian, he rejoined the Army, again as a captain. During his military career and hiatus, Hackworth accrued enough college credits to earn a Bachelor of Science in History from Austin Peay State University in 1964.

He went to Vietnam as a major in 1965, eventually forming Tiger Force with the intention to out-guerrilla the guerrillas. While Hackworth was still with the unit, he earned the Presidential Unit Citation. Hackworth was apparently the moral compass of the unit; after he left the unit, they went on to kill hundreds of noncombatants.

While still in the Army, Hackworth wrote *The Vietnam Primer* with General Marshall. The book recommended the use of guerrilla tactics in Vietnam. Hackworth and Marshall went on an Army-sponsored tour across the country, promoting the book and the war. After the tour he received a promotion to lieutenant colonel.

REFLECTIONS ON LEADERSHIP

During the tour and his subsequent Pentagon duty, Hackworth began to question American involvement in Vietnam. Despite this, Hackworth ended up back in Vietnam with an opportunity to test his counter-insurgency theories. He took an underperforming unit and turned it into a Recondo Unit (RECONnaissance and commanDO).

Next, Hackworth served with a South Vietnamese ARVN unit. His experiences there created more friction with the Army. Despite this, he received a promotion to colonel and orders to attend the Army War College, which is usually a step toward promotion to general. Hackworth declined the opportunity to attend the war college.

He eventually appeared on a television interview show, condemning the war and urging the United States to withdraw. Soon after, Hackworth retired from the Army. There were rumors and accusations that among other things he ran gambling houses and brothels in Vietnam. He was nearly court-martialed, but Secretary of the Army Robert Frohlke decided not to press charges. This was most likely due to several factors, including his career accomplishments. There was also the fear that proceeding with a prosecution over suspected misdeeds might seem like the Army was trying to punish an outspoken war hero.

Again, we have a case of someone with undeniable leadership skills and abilities, but who *may* have had issues in other areas of his life.

The first thing to remember here is that the claims against Hackworth were not substantiated. We do not know what happened and probably never will.

Second, it sometimes seems that the passions that make some people great and give them extraordinary abilities and genius in their field cause them to become frustrated with those who cannot see and recognize their genius, especially when those who cannot see are in a position of power over them. These geniuses sometimes have difficulty reining in that passion.

Hackworth's quote is blunt, and may even be aimed at those who could not see his genius. "If you find yourself in a fair fight, you didn't plan your mission properly." Hackworth is telling the Pentagon that they did not plan their mission in Vietnam properly. He tells them this many times and many ways, and he finally becomes frustrated and retires, though not quietly.

Despite this, the quote is accurate. Hackworth wants you to do your research. He wants you to find your opponent's strengths and weaknesses; he also wants you to know your own strengths and weaknesses. Knowing these things and

REFLECTIONS ON LEADERSHIP

the nature of the mission, you should be able to plan and strategize so that you take on the mission with an overwhelming advantage.

Hackworth wants you to take on a mission you know you can win. If with your first reconnoiter you realize you cannot win, withdraw and do more planning. Keep this cycle up until you know that you will not be entering a fair fight.

Perhaps when dealing with the Pentagon, he failed to follow his own advice.

Leadership is a gift. It's given by those who follow. You have to be worthy of it."

General Mark Welsh

W elsh is a former Chief of Staff of the United States Air Force, who retired in 2016 after over 40 years of service.

Welsh captures something here that many miss. Leadership, true leadership, not leadership granted by rank, is bestowed upon leaders by followers. People choose who they will follow. Anyone can hold a rank that puts them in a position of authority over others; that does not make them a leader. What makes them a leader is having followers, people who have willingly put themselves in the hands of another.

REFLECTIONS ON LEADERSHIP

People follow those who have shown that they care about and want the best for those who would follow. Anyone can bark orders, but a leader has learned to ask for your trust. When people choose to follow you, they have placed trust in you. You have to be worthy of that trust.

Here are some questions you can ask yourself to determine if you are worthy of leadership.

Is your leadership for your gain or for the gain of all? If your motivation for leadership is selfish, then you are doing it for the wrong reasons, and your followers will know. People are smart and they can sniff out self-serving behaviors. Everything you do, every action, should be a reflection of your vision for the team. It should be a vision that the team shares and is working toward also. A true leader is concerned for the wellbeing of their followers and places that wellbeing above their own. When a leader puts their all into their followers, their followers will put their all into their leader.

Do you cover up your fears or do you seek answers? Fears are normal. Fears are a sign that you are not overconfident. It is what you do with those fears that sets you apart. If you try to bury those fears and pretend that they do not exist, you will likely fail as a leader. If you use your fears as a sign that you have a gap in your knowledge and seek to close that gap, then you are setting yourself up for success. A true leader knows that they do not know everything and are constantly learning to improve themselves.

When you are seeking to improve yourself, you are in a position to seek to improve your followers.

What am I doing every day to earn my leadership? Real leaders do not take their leadership for granted. Remember, a leader needs to work every day to show their followers that the leader is worthy of their trust. The leader must be a leader every day, not just those days when they feel like it. Leadership is not a convenience. Leadership is a lifestyle.

Is your leadership bringing out the best in others? Are you coaching and mentoring your followers or are you just getting work out of them? You can use a structured system or an informal system, but you have to ensure that when you and your followers part ways, they are better people for having known you.

Recommend books and magazines to your followers you have read. Share with them the lessons you have learned through podcasts and life. Find those teachable moments to impart wisdom. And always find time to just listen.

REFLECTIONS ON LEADERSHIP

Are you communicating your vision to your team with such clarity that they too want to achieve the vision? Like with so many other areas of life, communication is a key to leadership. You have to be able to clearly communicate your objectives. You have to clearly communicate your lessons. You have to clearly communicate your vision.

If you are not a good communicator or you lack confidence in your communication, find ways around it. You do not become a better communicator by being quiet. Join speaking groups whose members will help you gain confidence giving presentations. Take classes in writing. Start a blog and seek feedback from readers. Do whatever you have to do to be the communicator that your followers need to effectively carry out your vision.

Follow these tips and you will be worthy of the gift your followers have given you.

Everyone talks about building a relationship with your customer. I think you build one with your employees first."

Angela Ahrendts

Ahrendts was the Senior Vice President of Retail at Apple from 2014 until 2019, but she has not always been involved in technology.

She was born in Indiana, where she attended New Palestine High School. After high school, she earned a Bachelor's degree in merchandising and marketing from Ball State University, after which she moved to New York to pursue a career in fashion. She worked at Warnaco, then Donna Karan International. From there she moved to Henri

REFLECTIONS ON LEADERSHIP

Bendel, then Fifth & Pacific Companies as Vice President of corporate merchandising and design.

She moved to several other companies, each time accepting a promotion, eventually becoming CEO of Burberry. Ahrendts said that she did not model her approach based on any other fashion house; instead, she looked to world-class design influence, including Apple Inc.

In 2013, Apple announced that they would be adding Ahrendts to their executive team.

She has received many awards and accolades including appearing on Fortune 50's Most Powerful Women in Business six times.

To say that Ahrendts has extensive experience in retail is putting it mildly. She knows retail as well as any executive in America. So why does someone with her knowledge base say that building a relationship with your employees is more important than building a relationship with your customers? Because she knows that if you take care of your employees, they will take care of your customers.

Your employees are on the front lines with your customers. You cannot see your customers from your corporate office, but your employees work with customers every day. Whatever story you want to tell your customers, you cannot tell it from your office, no matter how loudly you say it. However, your employees communicate a story to your customers a thousand different ways every day. Make sure the story they are telling is your story.

Take care of your employees and they will be happy. If your employees are happy, your customers will feel it.

So how does a senior vice president of one of the largest tech companies in the world develop a relationship with her employees? She had several techniques. One of Ahrendts' moves at Apple was to redesign the retail stores. She was not focused on numbers, but on designing the stores to encourage social interaction. She focused on softer lighting and better displays for products. She wanted to make the stores resemble town squares.

Ahrendts envisioned Apple stores as being a meeting place. Her employees noticed her warmth, as she was in the habit of sending weekly video messages where she offered updates and encouragement. Employees like the messages, saying that they felt unscripted and natural.

She also launched a program where retail employees could work on special projects with corporate teams to provide advancement opportunities within the company.

REFLECTIONS ON LEADERSHIP

Ahrendts put a feedback system in place called Loop, where employees can share ideas with each other and the company. They can offer ideas to fix problems, and the company can respond to the employees about how they are fixing the problem.

For Ahrendts, it is not just about taking care of the employees; she also wants to hire the right employees. She looks for people with high emotional intelligence. In the interview, she listens to see if the candidate uses "I" statements or "we" statements. Does the candidate talk about their accomplishments or do they talk about the accomplishments of their teams?

Ahrendts did not arrive at Apple intending to make blanket changes across the retail division; not until she got to know the division and learned what worked and what did not did she start looking at changes. She could not do that without first getting to know the culture, and to get to know the culture, she had to get to know the employees.

In her first month on the job, she visited stores in San Francisco and London and made plans to visit Tokyo and other stores in the coming weeks.

In a memo she sent to her employees after the first month on the job, she stuck to her own thoughts on hiring employees, talking about "the team" and "we."

In the first two paragraphs of the memo, she connects with the employees by thanking them for their kind words, and she praises them for the job they are doing.

The third paragraph starts, "Looking to the future …" This is where she communicates her vision to her followers. In her vision, she talks about "customer journey," "changing how customers shop," and "customer experience." She is clearly communicating to her followers the importance of the customer. She uses "we," "us," and "our" to show her followers that helping the customer and creating the vision is a team effort.

Ahrendts said that customers "still want to feel surprised and delighted by the personalized Apple experience we provide at every turn." There is more in the memo about her vision, but this passage clearly sums up her vision: She and her followers are a team and that every customer is to be treated like an individual rather than as one of many.

Ahrendts clearly understands that her relationship with her followers, her team, improves Apple's relationship with its customers.

"If we treat people as they are, we make them worse. If we treat people as they ought to be, we help them become what they are capable of becoming."

Johann Wolfgang von Goethe

Von Goethe was a man of many talents. He was a poet, a novelist, a playwright, a philosopher, and a civil servant from Germany. He wrote many books including *Theory of Colors* and the famous book *Faust*.

People who respect you will try to be how you see them. Telling someone that they are good at something helps create a self-fulfilling prophesy.

Treating people a certain way shows them how they ought to act. If we treat people a certain way, they act a certain way.

One of the best-known examples of how one person's behavior changes another person's self-perception is the Pygmalion effect. The effect is named after a Greek legend about a king and sculptor who fell in love with a statue he carved. He made an offering to Aphrodite during Venus's festival day. During the offering, he declared his love for the statue.

The Pygmalion effect describes the act of giving life to something that was not real to begin with.

In a well-known experiment, teachers were told that some of their students had a high IQ. In reality, the students were chosen by random.

At the end of the school year, those students showed improved IQ scores. There are several ways to look at this study, and some people argue the original study results were flawed. Others studies claim that the original had some things going for it.

Put simply, the Pygmalion effect says that if you expect more out of a person, the better the person will perform. This is a shocking revelation, I know. I am sure all of you can think of times that you have experienced this yourself. You have probably seen children, teens, spouses, employees, yourself, and others who have improved after an authority figure gave the person a compliment or a vote of confidence that the person could achieve a goal or complete a difficult task.

Today we often call these stretch tasks or assignments, as the person is close to having the necessary skills to complete a task and by the time they are done, they will have experienced enough growth and development to complete it.

Stretch tasks are just one way to expect more out of your followers. Be tactical in how you determine which stretch assignments to assign to them. Work with the follower to determine their goals and together you can determine what areas they should focus on to help them achieve the goals.

The plan should include specific assignments, measurements for success (remember, not all forms of success can be measured in numbers), and timelines. As a leader, you need to be available to the follower to coach, guide, and mentor. You may even consider finding another follower of yours, who has skills and abilities more advanced than this follower, and use this as a stretch assignment for them.

All of this may seem like a lot of work, but consider the costs of lost productivity from unmotivated, uninspired staff and the costs of hiring, onboarding, and training versus the costs of keeping a follower you were able to help become what they are capable of being.

The second part of this quote is not much of a revelation or it shouldn't be. Treat people a certain way and they start to act and think that way. Has anyone ever told you that you were good at a task or a skill that you did not recognize on your own? What happened afterward? Chances are you started paying attention to that skill and working on it.

This tactic also works with your followers.

Treat people like they are a better person and they begin to act like a better person. Looking at yourself, if someone has confidence is you, how does it affect your behavior? If you respect that person (even if you don't), chances are you notice a boost in your confidence. We should spend our time building each other up.

The first part of the quote is often rendered as "When we treat people as they are, they will remain as they are." I like the quote above better. Not only is this version inaccurate as a quote, it is also inaccurate in life. People do not remain the same. People always change. Sometimes the change is to get better. Sometimes the change is to get worse.

REFLECTIONS ON LEADERSHIP

If we do nothing to make a person better, we are making them worse through benign neglect. Every time you leave a team, a place, a follower, your goal should be to leave them better than when you found them.

That is the sign of a leader.

Action Steps

Developing a coaching program for your follower is really pretty easy. Establish a goal with the follower. There is no need to go all SMART on the goal. SMART can be useful, but people argue about what the letters mean, they get too hung up on semantics, and they lose sight of the important thing: actually doing the goal. Do ensure there is a measurable result and a deadline.

Together, brainstorm several objectives for reaching the goal, and settle on one or two..

Create a strategy for each. Attend a class, read a book, etc.

Create a tactic for each. Have the follower attend the class, read the book, etc.

Meet with the follower to discuss their results, and start over. These meetings need to occur at least every other week, if not weekly. If the follower needs feedback or help (the class is several months away or the book is backordered), have the follower report back to develop an alternate course of action. This is easily achievable during your weekly one-to- ones.

You have having one-to-ones with your followers, right? If not, see page 8 for a brief explanation.

A leader is not an administrator who loves to run others, but someone who carries water for his people so that they can get on with their jobs."

Robert Townsend

This is not Robert Townsend the actor; this is Robert Townsend the author and business man. Townsend worked his way through the ranks of American Express until he left as the senior vice president for investment and international banking. He left in 1962 to become the CEO of Avis Car Rental. For the first time in its history, the company began to turn a profit. Townsend attributed the turnaround to Theory Y.

Theory X and Theory Y is a management theory advanced in the 1950s by MIT professor Douglas McGregor. In Theory X, managers believe that their employees are less intelligent, lazy, and motivated only by a paycheck. These managers believe their followers need to be supervised through two different supervisory styles. One is the close supervision style; the other style was for the manager to stay away from the employee, who would somehow become motivated to work. (For the record, McGregor felt the best approach for a Theory X manager was somewhere in between.)

Theory Y managers believe that employees are driven by intrinsic motivation that managers need to tap into. These managers do not provide close supervision, but are available to their employees to approve the project. Theory Y managers aim for a closer relationship with their employees by looking for more of a coaching and mentoring relationship with them.

Townsend's quote is an example of servant leadership. Theory Y is a natural vehicle to use as a servant leader. Upon leaving Avis, Townsend became an author, speaker, and talk show guest. He was particularly critical of CEOs who put profits above people. He believed that if CEOs got out of the way of their people, the profits would come.

REFLECTIONS ON LEADERSHIP

Author Robert K. Greenleaf invented the term "servant leadership" in 1970. Greenleaf is certainly not the creator of the idea of being a servant leader, nor is Townsend. You have seen many quotes in this book from leaders far older than Townsend that all, in one way or another, point to the idea of servant leaders.

Townsend was not the first to adhere to this type of leadership theory, but he summed it up well with this quote. Now, if you will excuse me, I have some water to carry.

If we win the hearts and minds of employees, we're going to have better business success."

Mary Barra

Mary Barra is General Motors' current CEO, and in 2015 she was listed as the number one in *Fortune*'s Most Powerful Women list. Barra has spent her adult life at General Motors. At 18 she worked for them inspecting hoods and fenders to pay for college. She went to college at General Motors Institute, now Kettering University, earning a Bachelor of Science degree in electrical engineering. In 1990, she earned an MBA from Stanford, on a General Motors fellowship.

When Barra speaks about winning "hearts and minds," she knows of what she speaks. General Motors has invested

REFLECTIONS ON LEADERSHIP

a lot of time and money in her, winning over her heart and mind. She has rewarded them with many years of service and is now considered one the best CEOs in General Motors history.

Louis Hubert Gonzalve Lyautey used the phrase "hearts and minds" regarding the Black Flags Rebellion of 1895. John Adams used it in 1818 when talking about the American Revolutionary War. The phrase even goes back to the Bible, though the context is different.

So how do you win people's hearts and minds? People search for causes; people want to be a part of something.

You can provide them that by showing them the vision of your organization. Show them how the vision affects them. People need meaning; they often spend time looking for it. In some cases, organizations can provide it.

Tell them what to do. People do not know what to do. You don't believe me? Try this. Ask your friends what their goals are. You will probably get responses like, make it to retirement, buy a boat, watch my team win the bowl thing.

Even when you press them for more substantial life goals, you are likely to see a confused look on their face. Many people do not have goals because they do not know what to do, even in their job.

Ask your friends what their job is and can they give you a title. Ask them what that entails, and they are likely to stare at you like you have just asked them what their goals are. Sure, they can tell you some duties. They can tell you their daily activities, but what is their job?

Next, ask the friend's boss what your friend's job is. The explanation may be a little less vague, but only a little, but the two definitions of the jobs are likely to be different.

People want definition, they want clarity, they want to know what to do, and they do not even know what that is in their jobs.

If you want to earn your followers' hearts and minds, start by setting clear expectations about their jobs.

Now, tell them how to do it. Explain how they can meet those expectations. You do not want them to be mindless robots following your orders, so do not give them a step-by-step guide, but tell them how to meet your expectations.

Last, tell them why they are doing the job. What is it about this job that needs to be done so the team can achieve its vision? People need to connect to others; that's why social media is so popular. People feel like they are being social animals by connecting with others online, but these are largely hollow connections. (I know that some people make lasting, real connections on social media. I have seen it, but you cannot tell me that you personally know all of your 500 followers. In fact, anthropologists suggest it is impossible to maintain connections with more than 150 people.)

Show your followers how their work directly impacts the goals of the organization, and they give you their hearts and minds. If the organization's goal is closely aligned with a follower's goal, they will work for your organization forever and may end up being one of your most valuable employees.

You do not believe me? Ask Mary Barra.

Action Steps

The fatal flaw of this approach is if your organization's culture (the sum total of its behaviors) is not in alignment with the vision, mission, and values of the organization, staff will not believe any of your eloquent vision speeches.

Culture begins with executives and managers, though all employees play a role. If you want to win the hearts and minds, align your actions with the vision, mission, and values of your organization.

Leadership is about vision and responsibility, not power."

Seth Berkley

Berkley is an epidemiologist and CEO of the GAVI Alliance. The original name was Global Alliance for Vaccines and Immunization. It has since shortened its name, but the mission is the same. It is a public-private partnership dedicated to increasing access to immunization in poor countries. Berkley became the CEO in 2011, after having founded and being the CEO of the Global Alliance for Vaccines and Immunization.

If you have to use positional power to get people to follow you, you are not a leader, you are a dictator. Real leaders have a vision they convey to their followers, one that is so compelling that followers want to follow. The leaders are responsible; they have to be, as they hold the lives of followers in their hands. Sometimes literally as in combat, law enforcement, and fire departments to name a few, but even if you are not sending your followers into life-threatening conditions, the environment your followers work in has a lot to do with the environment your followers live in, away from work. The stress from working in a toxic environment has huge impacts on the lives of followers.

Many organizations preach wellness and work/life balance, but if an employee enjoys their job, enjoys going to work each day because they know that their peers and their managers love them and care about their wellbeing, why do organizations need to be worried about work/life balance?

The idea of work and life balance to maintain mental health implies that our life is a safe place and our work is not. That's a sad commentary. Some work environments are going to be unsafe or have the potential for danger: prisons, factories, battlefields. There's only so much you can do in those environments to mitigate those environmental work hazards. Tactics, training, and camaraderie are among the best ways to mitigate the dangers.

So if your followers work in hazardous conditions, and you know it, why would you resort to power get people to do what you want? Their jobs are already stressful enough; why would you make them even more stressful by being a dictator?

There are plenty of quotes in this book from known and noted military leaders, who suggest that even leading men off to their deaths does not require a dictatorial approach. In fact, according to these military leaders, your followers are better off without that kind of approach.

So you have a responsibility to use your vision to be the leader your people require.

Here are a few ways to communicate your vision to your followers.

Start by understanding them. You may know something about them, their job history, maybe some personal history, you may even know something about their family.

But do you know what motivates them? Do you know what their goals are? Do you know how this job helps them with their vision?

Until you know these answers, you will have a difficult time reaching your followers.

When you know what drives them, you will know how to reach them. You can target your message to them. You can

REFLECTIONS ON LEADERSHIP

tell them how your vision relates to them and how it helps them reach their goals.

Tell your followers what actions they need to take to achieve the goals. Work with your followers to develop the plans, including steps, measures of success, and deadlines.

Stay out of their way. Once you have agreed with your followers what the plan and goals are, stay out of their way and allow them to get the job done. Haul water for them and clear any barriers out of their way; give them coaching and encouragement.

Responsibly use your vision to lead your followers.

Leaders aren't born; they are made. And they are made just like anything else, through hard work. And that's the price we'll have to pay to achieve that goal, or any goal."

Vince Lombardi

Lombardi knew something about hard work. He worked his way through many coaching jobs, always improving, and looking for his break. Finally, he arrived in Green Bay. The 1958 season saw the Green Bay Packers with a 1-10-1 record, the worst in the Packers' history.

In 1959, Lombardi brought the team to a 7-5 record, and he was named the Coach of the Year. He was known for being tough on his players, but he was also known to have

REFLECTIONS ON LEADERSHIP

fully integrated his team, making rules that if a local restaurant would not serve any of his players, then the restaurant would be off limits to all of his players. On the road, the team would only stay in hotels where all of his players could stay. He also let it be known that no one in his organizations would discriminate against gay staff or players.

Lombardi may have been hard on his team, but it seems to have been in the name of getting the best from them.

Where so many of these quotes have been focused on the work leaders need to put into their followers, we are turning our attention to the work leaders need to put into themselves.

I have been a supervisor for over 12 years. I am not the same leader now that I was when I started. I have learned a lot about leadership, and I will not stop learning about leadership. No matter your field of endeavor, you need to keep learning.

It's not going to be easy; I learned many hard lessons on the way. There were times that I realized later the mistakes I had made. There were times that for the sake of the team and my followers, I had to eat crow, make apologies, and smooth things over. Nearly everything I have learned about leadership I learned on my own or by observing others, both negative and positive examples.

Many organizations have training programs for leaders. My own organization sent me to such training. It was rudimentary and looking back at it, I see that the information I learned has proven to be wrong. That was when I first got promoted. I have not received any other training or coaching from the organization since; the only training classes or coaching available are for first-time supervisors.

Hopefully, your organization has a formalized training program for leaders. Even if your organization does have a training program, though, it would be beneficial to you and your followers if you sought other training, self-directed and otherwise.

I started looking at the supervisors and managers I liked, and I asked myself what they did that made me like them. There were several, but one stood out head and shoulders above the rest. I spent a lot of time observing him while working for him. I learned lessons about leadership I did not fully understand until years later.

Just because he was a good leader did not mean he was liked by everyone or was even the perfect leader. Some of his followers did not like him because he was quick-witted and could twist a person up in a debate before people even knew they were in a debate. He was good at letting people

REFLECTIONS ON LEADERSHIP

know when they were wrong, but he was also good at providing solutions.

When I had a house fire, I learned he was a servant leader (even if I did not yet know what a servant leader was). He knew I am a private person and not likely to ask for help. He assigned one close friend of mine to be the point of contact for anyone asking information about how I was doing and what I needed. He found out some of our immediate needs, then texted those needs out to followers he knew wanted to help.

One day I was venting to him about how all of our pots and pans had been destroyed. I was sincerely venting, not expecting anything. He let me vent, then I went to work. Soon, one of my followers came into work on his day off with a five- or six-piece pan set under his arm.

I asked what he was doing. He said that this manager sent out a group text saying what I needed. He handed me the box, and went off to enjoy the rest of his day off.

That was a turning point for me. He and I (through his mentorship) had created a work environment where everyone trusted each other so much that we took care of each other outside of work, not just at work.

Besides learning from the good examples, there were plenty of bad examples to learn from. I began treating followers the opposite of the way these examples were treating followers.

Eventually I felt that I needed formal training in leadership. I am not telling you that you have to have formal training to be a leader, but it was the route I chose for both personal and professional reasons. I enrolled in school and eventually earned a Master of Science in Management and Leadership degree.

I thought the hard work was getting my degree. In reality, the hard work was trying to help a system that did not want the help. I kept working anyway.

The hard work I did not anticipate was after I accepted another job, and my followers and peers told me how much I had impacted their lives and careers and how sad they were to see me go, but how glad they were for me.

My hard work did eventually pay off, just not for the organization I had desperately wanted to help.

Action Steps

There are many routes to learning; mine was through formal education, although I do not think you need a formal education. It's entirely up to the individual and their chosen

REFLECTIONS ON LEADERSHIP

field. If you do not want to spend the years earning a degree, many universities are offering shorter certificate programs.

Outside of formal education, look for books, videos, magazines, and podcasts. Also look for conferences and seminars.

Finally, finding mentors and coaches is always a good idea. They do not have to be in your field to provide valuable lessons.

The final test of a leader is that he leaves behind him in other men the conviction and the will to carry on."

Walter Lippmann

Lippmann was considered by many to be the father of modern journalism. I will try not to hold that against him. In his defense, his window of journalism was in the 1950s and 1960s. I do not suppose he can be blamed for the modern view of journalism where the perception is that you take sides and sling mud at people you do not like and turn a blind eye to the people you do like.

Again, here we have someone who is difficult to put a finger on. Lippmann was an avowed socialist in his early years, serving as the president of the Harvard Socialist Club

REFLECTIONS ON LEADERSHIP

and a member of the Executive Committee of the Intercollegiate Socialist Society.

Initially, he supported Franklin Roosevelt and his New Deal. He even urged Roosevelt to assume dictatorial powers. By the end of Roosevelt's presidency, Lippmann had become disillusioned with Roosevelt, claiming that the president's attempted manipulation of the Supreme Court was a threat to the American Constitutional system.

Lippmann himself seemed to be aware of the threat of journalism and the power it held over the people. He recognized that public policy was becoming complex and that most people were too busy to dedicate the time required to be fully aware of all public policy decisions.

He believed that the problem of democracy was the accuracy of news and protection of sources. He believed that people made up their minds before obtaining the facts, which was the threat to democracy. (Sound familiar?)

Whatever his politics, Lippmann was on to something with his quote on leadership. This quote is about legacy. A good leader's legacy will inspire people to continue the leader's vision, even after the leader is gone.

I spoke in the previous entry about my departure from an organization. I am in no way saying that my leadership skills qualify me for any special recognition. I am simply trying to do the best I can for my followers; they get full credit for any of their successes.

On the day that I announced to my followers that I was moving on, they sent me messages that spoke about the impact I had on their lives and careers and the message was clear: They were going to continue on with my coaching and mentorship after I was gone.

That same day, one of my peers contacted me to ask my advice about problems he was having with his staff. He put aside his ego and admitted that his staff were having problems with him. He had the courage to admit that some of his followers were leaving him for reasons other than days off and different shifts.

I gave him advice and areas to work on. I talked to him about trust and vulnerability. I told him about coaching, mentoring, and delegating. I advised him against the long lectures I know he prefers in favor of breaking concepts into small, digestible chunks.

I then mentioned one of his staff members. My job at this time was to work in my peers' positions while they were on vacation, sick, or in training. I had several opportunities to work for him, and I knew his followers well.

REFLECTIONS ON LEADERSHIP

My peer told me that he had a hard time motivating this staff member. He often found him "sitting on his ass," and that he had to keep on him to keep him working. I offered suggestions to motivate the staff member that did not involve typical goals, such as pay and promotions.

Then I had to tell my peer that I had never witnessed this behavior from his follower. I had seen just the opposite. For me, the follower was a hard worker who kept himself busy and needed little supervision.

My role was to fill the hole. When I filled in for one of my peers, I was not there to make changes or to shake things up. My role was to keep the ship afloat until my peer returned to their post.

I told this follower as much. I told him that he is in charge of his area, and I am just there to help. I, in essence, told him that I trusted him to make decisions, so he did. His supervisor takes a different approach. He makes decisions for his follower, so the follower stopped making decisions.

I ask nothing of him and he gives me everything.

My peer sat silent for a long time. I kept quiet waiting for him to speak. He clearly did not know what to make of this idea of "doing nothing" to get the best out of his followers.

I know this peer well. I know him to be analytical. I also know that in the past, when I have given him advice, he processed and followed through with it.

My hope is that in my absence, he will have the conviction to carry on with my advice, so that one day he will know the pleasure of asking nothing from a follower, and receiving everything.

Action Steps

Ask yourself if you are thinking for your followers, or if they are thinking for themselves. If you find that your followers are reluctant to make decisions, take a look at your leadership. Let go of some of the decisions and trust your followers. If they can do a job 75 percent as well as you can, it's time to hand the task over to them.

I'm sure there are plenty of other things you can be doing.

REFLECTIONS ON LEADERSHIP

Leadership is in the eyes of other people; it is they who proclaim you as a leader."

Carrie Gilstrap

It does not matter what rank you are; if people do not follow you, you are not a leader. People choose who they follow. People may have to do what a person of higher rank tells them to do, but that does not make the person with the higher rank a leader. It makes them a ruler, a person exercising dominion.

A ruler may get followers to do work, but they cannot make them care about the work. A ruler cannot make followers put in their all; they can only make followers do enough to keep the ruler from bothering them.

Rulers have a hard time understanding why followers are not motivated, if they even pay it any thought. Everyone has some source of intrinsic motivation, something that makes the get out of bed in the morning, something that feeds them, feeds their soul. Some people work in places that feed their intrinsic motivation; many more do not. Even still, people whose job does not feed their intrinsic motivation can usually find something about their job that feeds them, something that keeps them going.

Rulers, by their toxic leadership style, drain all of that intrinsic motivation. The only way a ruler knows how to provide extrinsic motivation is through threats. They are incapable of providing positive feedback without adding at least one negative. Rulers do not know how to be positive with their followers; all they know is how to motivate through fear and intimidation.

After they have completely demoralized their followers, rulers are surprised when their followers lack intrinsic motivation, not realizing or caring that they have drained it from them.

Leaders want to make all around them better. Leaders want to lift people up; they want to improve the workplace. They want to improve processes. They want to make the organization better by making the followers better.

REFLECTIONS ON LEADERSHIP

Leaders know their followers' strengths, weaknesses, and goals. They also know these things about themselves. They know their followers' intrinsic motivation, so they know how to motivate through something more than threats.

Leaders find the good in everything. They are grateful and find a silver lining to everything. If you lose an account, that means you have time to develop new ones. Sales are slumping, but it gives you time to send people to training.

Leaders coach and mentor staff. They always want to create the next generation of leaders. They want to teach. They want people to learn and improve. Leaders want to train followers to replace them when they are gone.

Is it any wonder people choose leaders over rulers?

Acknowledgements

To my wife, Margo, without whom this book would not exist. We are quick to thank the military and first responders as they protect us from enemies foreign and domestic, and we should.

But let's not forget those families they leave behind. I have been deployed away from home for prison riots, forest fires, volcanoes, hurricanes and during COVID-19, for six weeks for response, and another four weeks for training, I am not sure how she does it.

Margo has maintained the farm, including building and maintaining fences, built a barn door and flower beds, adopted horses and dogs, planted and trimmed trees, and much more.

I am not naturally open and expressive. She is, and has somehow remained patient while I found my voice.

While thanking military and first responders, take a moment to thank their families. I couldn't do this without

REFLECTIONS ON LEADERSHIP

mine. She also supported the writing of this book, in the hopes that others may see what leadership looks like.

It was during these events and my work in corrections that I learned from positive (and negative) examples of what leadership can look like. While it would be entirely appropriate to mention some of those examples, I believe it is wholly more appropriate to thank those who followed, and in their following taught me more than positive examples of leadership could.

Listen to your followers and they will tell you more than any book ever could.

Thanks to my editor, Susan Rooks, who did her best to make me look and sound smart. She worked hard on this manuscript and brought the fresh eye to the project that I could not. She was also patient with me as the editing went much slower than it would have under normal circumstances. You see, I started working with her during COVID-19. I divided time between eastern and western Washington State helping with the response to this virus, which left me with little time or bandwidth to work on the manuscript. She patiently waited while I chipped out time here and there to complete it.

To Sarah Elkins, who told me about Susan. Sarah is a podcast host, author, and consultant. She teaches people how to unearth their stories and use them to get the most out of themselves. Her book and podcast are titled "Your Stories Don't Define You. How You Tell Them Will." She helped me realize that a person's past is less important than what you take from it. Frame your story one way, and you're the victim; frame it another and you are the hero. Be careful of the stories you tell yourself; they have a way of coming true.

About the Author

Dennis Mossburg has worked over 18 years in corrections and is an Incident Command System (ICS), Type III Operations Section Chief. Dennis is also the founder of Grey Moose Leadership Group.

As a leader, he has supervised the day-to-day activities and emergency responses of corrections staff. As a member of a Type III Incident Management Team, Dennis has responded to emergencies involving contaminated water incidents, computer system breeches, the Kilauea Volcano in Hawai'i, and Hurricane Florence in North Carolina.

Professionally, Dennis has led teams in preplanned uses of force in the corrections setting, supported county jails in communities under threat of wildfires, and most recently, Dennis has been deployed in Washington State to assist with COVID-19 response.

Much of his leadership experience has been in getting Type A personalities to get along and move in the same direction.

He is also a volunteer at Dachshund Rescue NW, the dog rescue owned by his wife, Margo, who not only rescues and adopts dachshunds, but also horses, donkeys and recently a hamster

Some of his proudest professional moments are helping to rescue the mistreated. Rescues also often end up helping families when they face life changes (divorce, military deployments, deaths in the family) that bring them to make choices that they do not want to make.

In his spare time, Dennis enjoys bicycling, weightlifting, and spending time with his wife and dogs. So far his battle-tested leaderships skills have no effect on the dogs or wife.

www.ingramcontent.com/pod-product-compliance
Lightning Source LLC
Chambersburg PA
CBHW071218080526
44587CB00013BA/1422